MADE IN
SWEDEN

Library of Congress Cataloging-in-Publication Data

Notini, Anja, 1940-
  Made in Sweden.

  Includes indexes.
  1. Decorative arts—Sweden—History—20th century. 2. Artists—
Sweden—Interviews. 3. Artists—Sweden—Biography. I. Title.
NK995.N6 1988 745'.0948588-1797
ISBN 0-88736-300-8

HERTFORDSHIRE
LIBRARY SERVICE

H50 243 933 0

Class 745.5'09485

Supplier AS | Price 19.95 | Date 12.88

FÖRLAGS AB WIKEN
© copyright Anja Notini 1987
Meckler Books, the trade division of Meckler corporation, 11 Ferry
Lane West, Westport, CT 06880
Meckler Ltd., Grosvenor Gardens House, Grosvenor Gardens,
London SW1W 0BS, England

All rights reserved. No part of this publication may be reproduced,
stored in a retrieval system, or transmitted in any form or by any
means, electronic, mechanical photocopying, recording or otherwise,
without prior permission of the publishers.

Photography: Anja Notini
Photograph of the author: Ralf Turander
Textual decoration: Madeleine Pyk
Layout: Paul Eklund and the author
Editor: Berit Erikson
Composition: Bokstaven
Printed in Italy 1988
ISBN 91-7024-401-4

Published with the
support of the Swedish Arts Council

Fly-leaf ill.: "A tie for Lennart",
woven fabric by Ann-Mari Forsberg
End-leaf ill.: "To Anja",
glass painting by Ulrica Hydman-Vallien

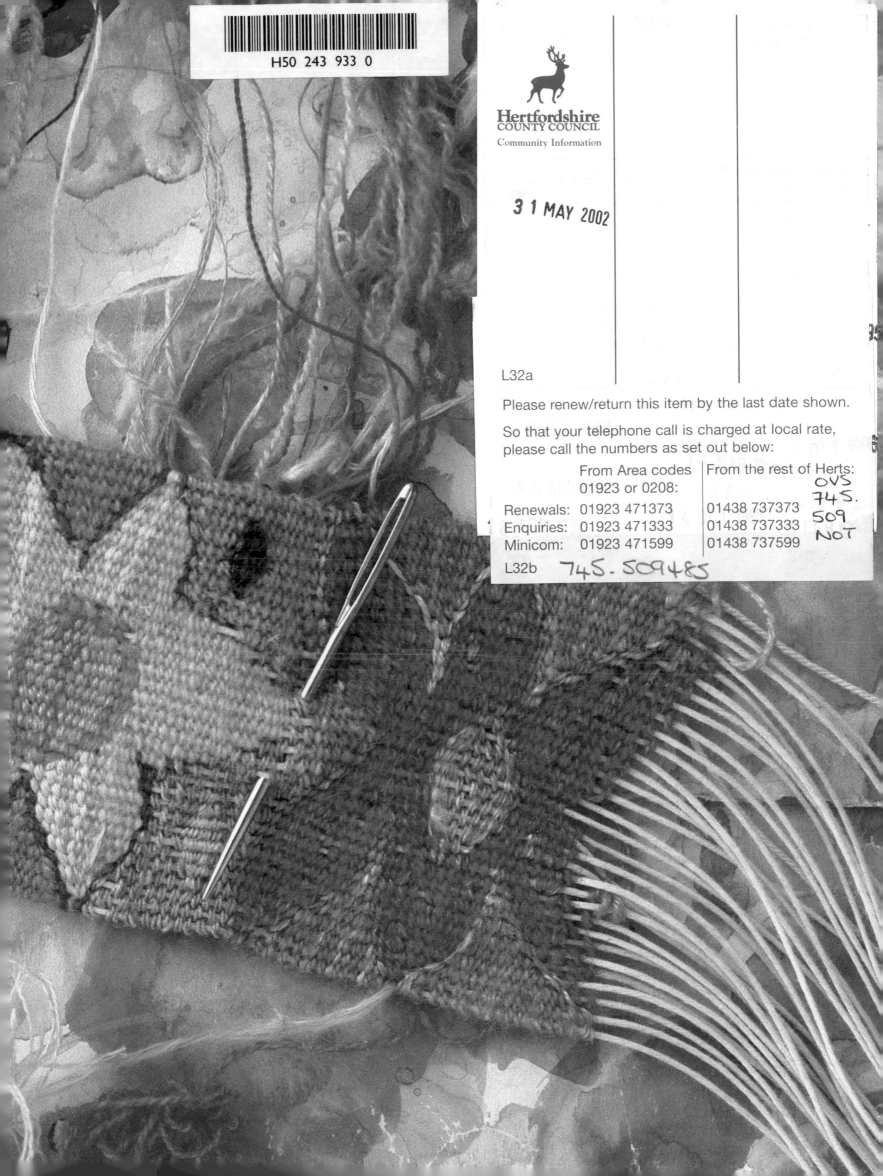

H50 243 933 0

Hertfordshire
COUNTY COUNCIL

Community Information

3 1 MAY 2002

L32a

Please renew/return this item by the last date shown.

So that your telephone call is charged at local rate,
please call the numbers as set out below:

From Area codes 01923 or 0208:	From the rest of Herts:
Renewals: 01923 471373	01438 737373
Enquiries: 01923 471333	01438 737333
Minicom: 01923 471599	01438 737599

OVS
745.
509
NOT

L32b   745.509485

ANJA NOTINI

MADE IN SWEDEN

ART HANDICRAFTS DESIGN

TABLE OF CONTENTS

N.B. The above list covers only the areas presented in this book.

"Happiness is the secret of beauty, the true substance of art. The artist, the poet, the musician bestow upon us, not their darkness, their suffering or their anxiety but a drop of pure light, eternal joy. And when entire peoples and languages attempt to probe the depths in their myths and religions, this joy is the utmost and the highest they can achieve."

Herman Hesse, *The Glass Bead Game*

PREFACE

BY NILS PETTER SUNDGREN

Is there any such thing as a Danish, Swedish, Italian, American, or Austrian "stylistic tradition"? Or does the spirit of the times mean more than any purely national heritage? Do today's artists and designers have more in common with their peers in other countries than with their Swedish predecessors? Or is there a national mainstream, an inheritance that survives the international fluctuations in style?

These questions easily arise when reading *Made in Sweden*. Many of the artists and craftsmen interviewed and exhibited here by Anja Notini are consciously seeking their roots in what is genuinely "Swedish." At the same time, many of their works clearly bear a contemporary stamp.

Twenty or so years ago it was axiomatic to speak of the ascetic, restrained tradition of Swedish 18th-century classicism, and its offshoots in our own century, "Swedish grace" and "Swedish modern." This is the tradition of pure lines, of cool beauty in which the extravagant yields priority to the functional.

Well into the 20th century, Sweden remained a poor country, sparsely populated by an agricultural people living in its deep forests and along its austere coasts. Poverty bred thrift and restraint. Styles such as Rococo and Empire, when they reached Sweden, were simplified and translated into simple materials like wood. Thrift also became a moral attitude, and one entirely in line with our puritan ethics. The classical interior of the Swedish manorhouse, with its large, wide rooms, broad floor planks, and its sparse grayish white furnishings, persisted for generations as our ideal.

The materials of the Swedish peasant culture are wood, wool, and iron. Swedish history contains no powerful nobility, or newly rich bourgeoisie, that could impress by its riches and magnificence, as was the case in Europe and England. The luxury articles that existed were purchased and imported from abroad.

In the 19th century Sweden, like other European countries, was influenced by the aesthetic idealism personified by Ruskin and Morris. The publication *The Studio* provided the inspiration for many Swedish homes, including Carl Larsson's Sundborn. Here as in other European countries people sought their way back to the simple beauty of a rustic culture, away from the machine-made vulgarities of Industrialism.

The slogan of this aesthetic movement in Sweden was "Beauty for all." For long periods of its history, Swedish design has reflected a democratic pathos, its primary concern being to create a good design culture and an attractive everyday environment for the masses. This attitude, deeply rooted in history, rendered Sweden particularly receptive to the Functionalism of the 1930s, which achieved a broader breakthrough here than elsewhere.

The 1980s have seen a revolt against Minimalism and Functionalism throughout the world. The slogan "Less is more" has been amended to "Less is a bore" – not only in architecture, but in the field of design as a whole. There now prevails a new, often entirely unrestrained, joy in shapes and colors, whether called Post-Modernist, Neo-Baroque, Neo-Kitsch or some other term. Designers are now working in strong, bold colors and new materials, performing breathtaking experiments that are light-years beyond the confines of traditional Swedish moderation and good taste.

But this fantasy, this delight in form, also has its traditions. Anja Notini's portrait interviews of living Swedish artists and craftsmen show how they seek their inspiration in folk art. Many of them display elements of Romanticism, a longing for an innocence of soul and of eye, beyond the Industrial or Post-Industrial society. One of the artists in this book says that he paints what is pristine, to express people's longing for the unspoiled. A young interior decorator creates an ample and generous easychair of crudely sawn pine, in contrast to the smart elegance of Italian tubular steel. "Anything homemade deserves respect—as does our traditional peasant furniture."

Many of the artists in this book come from a Swedish peasant tradition, to which they are seeking to return in order to carry the old traditions of craftsmanship onward. They revive half-forgotten crafts and patterns, select their own wool, and color the yarn with natural dyes. When Gocken Jobs creates her patterns from modest wildflowers, scrupulously and lovingly studied, she is associating directly to a heritage from Linnaeus. Others seek the magic of folklore. One textile artist describes how she finds inspiration in the deep, dark forests, which conjure forth strange forms, with thick undergrowth, mysterious trolls, and vast treetrunks.

This romantic love of Nature has deep roots. If Sweden today has any kind of generally accepted religion, it is a sort of Pantheism, a romantic absorption into the moods of Nature. In this, we are perhaps closer to the Japanese and Chinese than to the people of Europe. The more we lose our contact with history and with any exact knowledge of it, the more we tend to linger in the dream of a life of innocence in some bygone rural idyll. That no such idyll ever existed does not matter.

Even our traditional Swedish "kitsch" appeals to our sentimental feeling for Nature. Until quite recently, many Swedish homes were adorned—or disfigured—by what we call "Haymarket" art. This is very simply put-together pictures, often painted to standard patterns, portraying red wood cabins with white cornerjoints, with Swedish flags against a blue sky, or elk, delineated against dark, secretive forest lakes.

Made in Sweden is not about "kitsch," but about personal craftsmanship of a very high quality. One of the many observations made in the book is that the connection between poverty and aesthetic restraint is by no means self-evident. Simple materials often produce rich and colorful effects. Art and beauty provide a joy with which life, otherwise, is very frugal and barren. One Lapp woman interviewed puts this very well when she observes that the Lapps adorn their dresses more grandly and elaborately when the surrounding terrain is more severe.

"Maybe our love of beauty is so deep that the grimmest setting, the poorest circumstances, the most Spartan life can also produce the most brilliant flowers of them all."

FOREWORD

A tale can be told in a thousand ways, and a story about creative people and their work could be varied ad infinitum. Each choice assumes a shape, a breath, of its own. As one of the artists in this book says: "In the encounter between things, a language emerges."

A language also emerges in the encounter between tradition and new creative thinking, between male and female creativity, and between the basic material and the manner in which it is described. If *Made in Sweden* has captured anything of the creative energy that exists in such vast measure in our country, it is also a tale from the Swedish folklore of the 1980s.

The folktale, the myth, the passion, the feeling, the emotional side of human consciousness, are part of the natural order that we have to try to re-learn. The romantic, irrational world of prehistoric man has time and again been rejected by Reason and Fact, but has always risen anew in fresh guise—for the simple reason that we need it. And since our contacts with our true desires and longings frequently take place through the intermediation of gifted people in the artistic professions, these people must be allowed to express themselves. They must be given the support, the recognition, and the freedom that will enable their creative powers to flourish.

Artistry and Quality are ultimately inner properties, to which some people can lend shape also in an outward, concrete form—a form that is constantly changing. Reality is also, I think, an experience. But one cannot *establish* reality, measure it, or weigh it. It has a life that is as fluid and composite as water. In the fraction of a second in which the picture is taken and the word written, the reality changes its light, its colors, its expression; so that any attempt to describe creative Sweden becomes a folktale. This book contains a colorful mixture of deadly seriousness and unrestrained hilarity, popular taste and "fine art," subtle aesthetics and a "slap-the-paint-around" approach—and any true story about Sweden must contain all of this.

ANJA NOTINI

HERTHA HILLFON

POTTER

Hertha Hillfon has been described as "a pioneer" of Swedish ceramic sculpture. When as a young girl she presented her drawings at a school of painting, she was told that there was "not much point in you training as an artist, young lady—and in any case you're bound to get married and have a family."

Which indeed she did—as can be both seen and felt in her pottery.

Today, everyday pictures that have engraved themselves in her memory are often turned into sculptures: a few eggs in a bowl, a white cloth, a pair of trousers thrown over a chair, and bread that acquires rounded, fragrant contours in the clay.

Herta continues to sculpt figures in the baking dough. "The dough rises and the clay shrinks," she says. "I did a lot of baking as a child, especially at Christmas and Easter; we were a big family, so the bread was necessary, but at the same time it was a game. Even then I made figures out of the dough. As a potter I substituted clay for the dough, and went on baking."

Hertha affirms the qualities of everyday life emphatically and with a distinct vocabulary. Van Gogh once said that no real painter could look in vain for something to paint within a yard or so of where he was standing. Hertha sculpts a pair of feet, a kitchen knife on a chopping board, a face, a coat, a round loaf of bread or Swedish coffee cake. She creates utility ware—though the milk jug is larger and heavier than the standard product, and so is the ladle. By enlarging the familiar, she makes us see it in a new light—and in wonderment. The white doves—all 20 of them—fly around her studio, out of the bread and into the pottery. Hertha says: "In the encounter between things, a language comes into being: the bowl, the ladle, the dove, the bread."

Hertha Hillfon.

Overleaf: The studio, designed by Gösta Hillfon, built in 196

The Chair—*polished, unglazed earthenware, 1985.*

The Dove, *unglazed pale earthenware, 1975.*

The pastry board.   *Ceramic still life.*

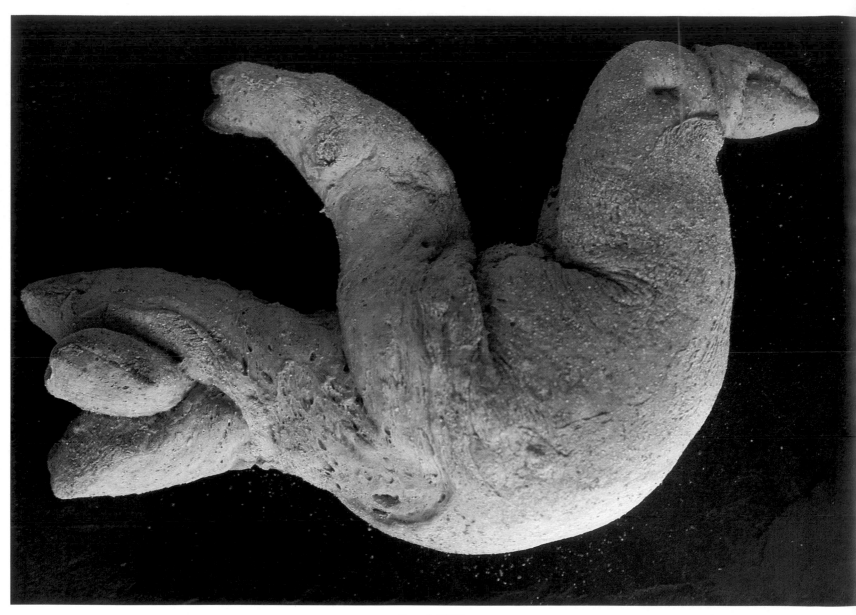

Bread, 1985.

Bread, 1985.

ANN-MARI FORSBERG

PICTORIAL WEAVER

A very special atmosphere surrounds Ann-Mari Forsberg's textile compositions. The largest can be seen in public institutions and company premises all over Sweden, in museums both here and abroad and, last but not least, in the two large pictorial tapestries in Uppsala Cathedral depicting 14 episodes from ecclesiastical history.

Ann-Mari's great tapestries are full of fragrance, flavor and mysterious movement. They remind the viewer of fairy tales and mysticism, of early Swedish history and, perhaps, of a magnificent, wide-open embrace, that beckons "come here . . . never forget . . . this is how beautiful life can be!"

As an artist she is at the same time extremely modern and a custodian of tradition. This applies equally to her technique and to her design. She enjoys talking about the artists who help create her major commissioned works, those who weave her sketches. Ann-Mari often shows them a full-scale painted sketch and a working description in a transparent woven fabric, with the contours drawn and marked with pins underneath the warp, shining through in a pattern.

"They usually work in pairs, so as to have plenty of room to sit weaving side by side. I come in to look once every week or so; my weavers are living with and in the picture, and I mustn't disturb them too much. They are superb artists, constantly creating. The big *Pharmacy of the Scent of Roses* tapestry has been woven four times, and each time the result is different.

"My weaves are so time-consuming, and we have been known to start the big ones in the autumn, weaving all through winter and spring, to finish some time in the early summer. I'm glad to have had the chance of getting so many done, because today the craft is fighting for its life. A few years ago we worked out that one square meter cost about SEK 20,000, if the weaver was to be paid a reasonable wage. For my own part, more often than not I have had to make do with the joy of seeing the picture emerge. My teacher Elsa Flensburg once told us when we were students that we were unlikely to make much money, but at least we would never be bored."

Ann-Mari's own kitchen is always fragrant with the smell of newly baked "Mazarine" buns and roasted Seville oranges.

Detail of a tapestry, Pharmacy of the Scent of Roses, *woven in 1964 by Birgit Elmstam and Eva Ekeblad in their workshop. The chemist himself bears a certain resemblance to Ann-Mari's father, who was a chemist in Vetlanda, where Ann-Mari grew up.*

Ann-Mari Forsberg spends her summers on the Baltic island of Gotland, where the weaving shop is full of shimmering colored yarns. Almost invariably, she starts a new weave by "sitting and doodling at the loom."

Tapestry variant, Pharmacy of the Scent of Roses, *woven in 1964. When Ann-Mari was a child in Vetlanda, pharmacies were still exciting places where medicine was made. The air was fragrant with ether and licorice, fruit and flowers. Even the dispensary had an exciting smell about it. The apothecary's jars were hand-thrown lidded pots, and the shop had beautiful wooden cabinets.*
Woven by Birgit Elmstam and Eva Ekeblad in their workshop. Now at Pharmacia, Uppsala. 210 × 350 cm.

Tapestry The Family Bakery, *woven in 1969 by Anita Dahlin and Sara Richter of Märta Måås-Fjetterström AB, at the Stockholm workshop. Baking croquembouche with the flag flying, ginger biscuits and fancy biscuits. While work was in progress, Ann-Mari baked all the cakes in the picture for her weavers "to keep them in the right mood." Commissioned by the Pågens family bakery.*
Now at Pågens Familjebageri in Malmö. 167 × 375 cm.

Detail from The Family Bakery, *woven in 1969.*

SUNE ENOKSSON

SAAMI (LAPP) CRAFTSMAN

Sune Enoksson is one of the most skilled Saami (Lapp) craftsmen in Sweden today. The beauty and variety of his own collection are dazzling. At home in his workshop he creates mostly knives, ranging from long ones (30–40 cm) to short ones which he calls "snub-nose."

He believes that it takes about half a lifetime to learn the art of making these beautiful things. He began when he was "big enough to hold a knife." Like all Saami children, he learned how to live with a knife. Children made their own wooden toys, and they cut their bread and meat with a knife, which they carried with them everywhere.

For many Saami, life has changed character and they no longer carry knives with them in their everyday lives. But Sune does.

"When the time comes for the reindeer slaughtering, you may use two or three different knives, depending on the job. The big knife is used mostly for cutting brushwood, but you can also chop wood and butcher carcasses with it. My wife, Astrid, uses a knife just as much as I do; you'll often find us out in the forests and fields, hunting and fishing. Astrid is a Saami craftswoman and we collect our materials out in the wilds—plants for her yarn-dying, curly-grained birchwood for my knives and so on. We therefore, always, need knives."

A knife takes at least three days to make, with another four or five days for final adjustments. The very finest knives take just over two weeks to produce. Materials, shapes, and patterns all stem from a traditional background, but no two knives are ever alike.

"Sometimes I use the geometrical woven pattern from the southern Saami tradition, at other times the stylized floral decoration of the northern Saami. The patterns have age-old associations with the shape of the knives. There are also patterns common to both traditions, such as dotted and straight-line motifs.

"Today, I usually sell the best knives to collectors—they're getting too valuable to be used in everyday life. I've studied many trade courses, for instance at the Saami Folk High School in Jokkmokk, and the furniture-making course at the Kiruna Practical Vocational School. I trained as a craft teacher at Nääs and my finest teacher was Arthur Jillker, a legendary craftsman, unsurpassed in terms of style, shape, and ornamentation. Anybody who has handled a knife made by him is considered very lucky."

A selection of Saami knives with special steel blades. The handles are of reindeer horn, with pewter and curly grained birch trimmings. The leather sheath is of hand-cured cowhide, with a strap of woven reindeer hide. The curved shape of the sheath is to protect the body when the user bends or sits down. The decorated knives are used at festivals and gatherings. There would often be a plainer version to be hung from the belt for everyday use.

Sune Enoksson in traditional Saami costume.

Previous pages: Sune Enoksson with one of his hunting dogs. Hunting, fishing, and Saami crafts are the essence of his life in the Tärnaby mountain region.

Sune carving a piece of elk meat with one of his own knives. The steel blade has his name on it.

Knives crafted by Sune Enoksson, taken out of the sheath to do full justice to the beauty of the handles and blades. Saami craftsmen have taken everything except the actual blade from their natural surroundings: curly grained birch (protuberances on the root, trunk, or branches of the tree) and horn, bone and sinews from the reindeer. The sheath knife was the only tool used. With it the craftsman shaped and finished, inscribed, whittled, and jabbed to produce the patterns, which were then greased with fat and soot, and rubbed with alder bark dye to produce the contrasting effect.

BARBRO BÄCKSTRÖM

SCULPTOR

Barbro Bäckström carves in various materials and casts in bronze, iron fabric, and aluminum. It is perhaps her iron-fabric sculptures that are best known. Often called "net sculptures," they are made of an iron netting used in construction work and, among other things, for reinforcing plaster sculptures.

For many years now, Barbro has been carving bodies or parts of bodies in relief or, preferably, in free form which let in light all around. Although the netting is not pleasant to touch, the final form is most pleasant to the eye!

"I look for bodily shapes that at the same time will express a landscape. Formations of waves, sand, and rocks are related to the landscape of the body, and in the netting I can make an open, weightless sculpture which allows the light to permeate.

"There exists, if you look for it, the same profound sensuality in the landscape as in the body. The netting has no temperature, yet its structure creates vibrations."

The netting sculptures are transformed by the movement of daylight, and walking slowly around them, one finds that the three-dimensional effect offers room for new discoveries. Barbro works entirely alone in her studio, and never uses a model.

"I enjoy sketching and drawing—I've been fond of it ever since I was a student at the National College of Art and Design, but in the studio at home I am always in the room while I am working. If necessary I feel my own body—the movement of the arm at the shoulder blade, and so on; often I use anatomy textbooks and sometimes cut out pictures describing a movement. I never plan what I'm going to do—because things often never turn out as I imagined! I believe that the material sets the pace, with me following on behind, and sometimes amazing, amusing things happen which I could never have suspected. I know exactly when the sculpture is finished: first you have a load of material hanging there, but after some cooperation with me, the sculpture starts breathing on its own, and then I stop. This may all sound ethereal, but that is how it is when things are at their best."

The netting hovers in the air like a three-dimensional ink drawing. The sculptures have a profound graphic impact, thanks to the play of wires that has made them popular far beyond the ranks of the art buffs. Barbro's work is exhibited at about ten museums in Sweden, including the National Museum and the Museum of Modern Art in Stockholm. For one of her exhibitions the poet Jan Östergren wrote a wonderful poem ending:

"the warmth of a body's weight . . .
caught lightly in a butterfly net . . ."

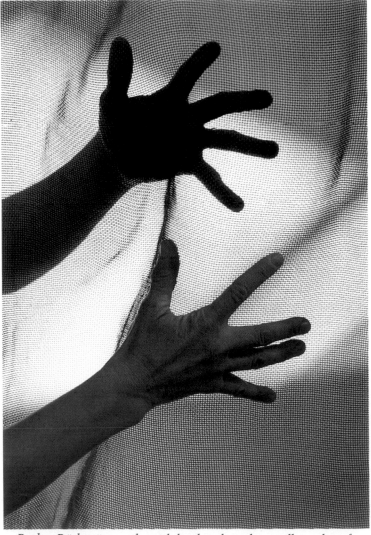

Barbro Bäckström works with her hands and a small number of tools, such as a hammer, when fashioning her iron fabric shapes.

28

Barbro Bäckström in her studio in Lund, 1986.

The sculpture on the wall is called Back, *and it is made of iron fabric. In the foreground,* Carrying—Carried, *is also of iron fabric, 1983 and 1982. The picture was taken during an exhibition at Waldemarsudde, Stockholm, in the spring of 1986.*

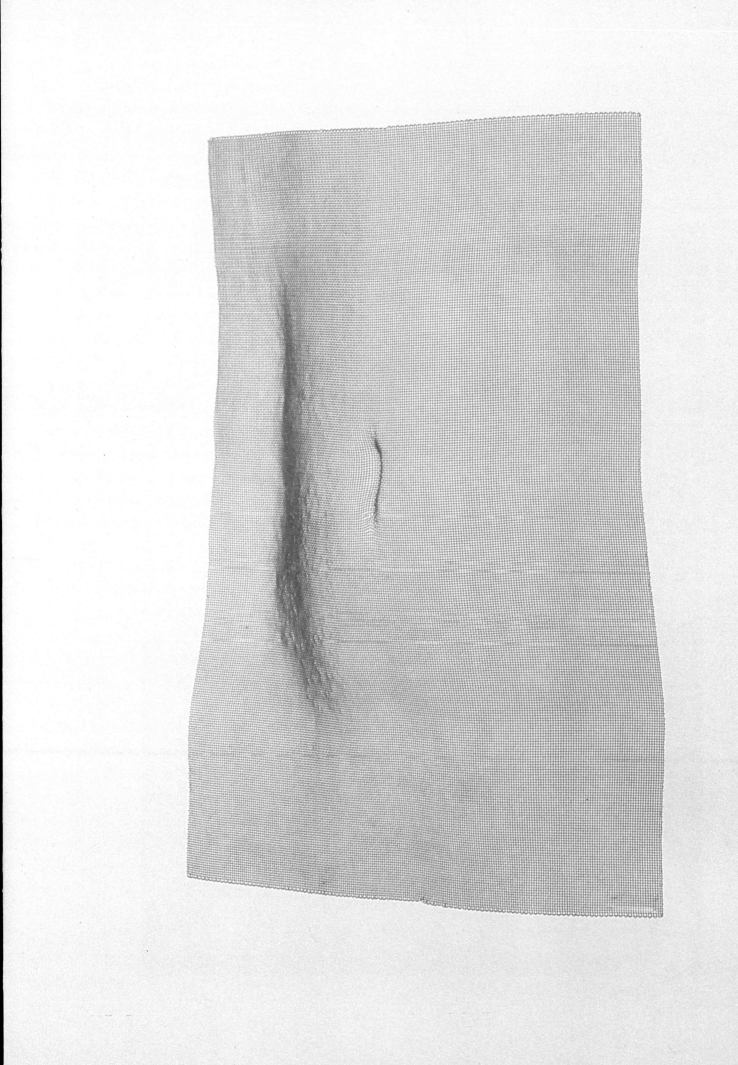

ARNE HÖGSANDER

PUPPET-MAKER

Arne Högsander makes theatrical masks of papier-mâché which are intense and expressive, encapsulating pain and evil, wisdom and beauty in an exquisite, controlled form. He contains his intensity within himself; it remains private until it emerges through the creativity of his hands. Or else it is concealed behind the mask for a part in the play, only blossoming out in the performance. Arne has produced theatrical masks for productions at the Stockholm Opera, the Stockholm Dramatic Theater, the Marionette Theater, Folkoperan and elsewhere.

"I thought I was going to be a graphic artist or painter, but instead became a puppet-maker and puppeteer. I needed the money to study at the National College of Art and Design, and I picked up a job in the Marionette Theater Workshop. There I learned to make dolls' masks out of papier-mâché. This was very interesting so I developed a technique to suit what I wanted to express.

"Although I only intended to *make* puppets, one day I was also needed on stage. Now I've been working for nearly 25 years with other people's scripts and ideas, but would like to concentrate more on experiments of my own. A puppet-maker, however, can't live on his trade alone. You must have a sideline, so I don't know if it will be possible."

Making your own masks calls for both vision and craftsmanship. Many people want to learn from Arne, and he has nothing against instructing them and teaching them his own technique.

The method is simple. After thinking about a dramatic part, Arne prepares sketches. "I make a plastellina model which I cover with tissue paper, paint with glue, dress up in wrapping paper and bond with plaster of Paris, before covering the whole thing with one more layer of glue and paper. Then I cut the model in two or three pieces so that I can take out the plastellina before gluing the parts together again. Sometimes I daub on a mixture of chalk, glue, and wood flour, and then paint the whole thing white. Finally I paint the decoration on in watercolors, and sometimes varnish it over with a coat of shellac."

Arne Högsander.

Animal masks for Folkoperan's production of Aida *in 1985. The cat is the goddess* Bast, *the falcon* Horus.

Various unpainted animal masks for productions at the Stockholm Dramatic Theatre and Opera, for example for the Opera production of Alban Berg's Lulu, which had its première in Stockholm in 1977.

INGELA HÅKANSSON-LAMM

TEXTILE DESIGNER

A day with Ingela is like walking into a modern book of fairy tales full of large, distinct pictures, whose proportions and colors make it supremely possible to transcend all normal limitations. Like Po-Po in the fairy tale following his kite straight through the mouth of the snap-dragon, you simply let yourself follow along, your eyes wide with wonder.

Ingela produces brightly colored fabrics with big black dots—and then adds a marzipan cake, with the same black Mickey Mouse dots. She creates ice-cream-colored patterns in cups and saucers that become all the more visible when a cake with the same pattern is placed on top.

One pattern has a huge green cowboy boot against a monochromatic background. The sofa in her living room is upholstered with a wide-striped, gray-and-black fabric. This is no ordinary living room.

Ingela says that friends have exclaimed, "My goodness, that's hideous—we had stuff just like it at home when I was small, and the bad taste of it was terrible," while others are delighted, and love the style.

"My first pattern," Ingela recalls, "came to me from a pillbox which I found on the subway. I'm always looking for things that look fantastic. Once, a house front I drew turned into a unique pattern. One of my 1950s vases made another. Everything I drag home, I regard as beautiful, and in no way superfluous. I love simplicity in diversity—I wish I could have a thousand polka-dot cups.

"When I was small I had a book called *Rufsi, Tufsi and Tott* about three small girls who always wore polka-dot dresses. They were incredibly beautiful and I never got tired of reading that book. Perhaps it left its mark."

Today Ingela has two daughters of her own, fairy-tale princesses in polka-dot dresses. She herself often sports a black bow with white dots.

A cake is frequently needed on many occasions: a children's party, a parents' meeting at the day nursery, an ordinary coffee break, or a dinner party. Ingela colors the marzipan and rolls it out, whisks up a salmon-pink or black cake mix from an American mail-order firm, squirts on whipped cream colored pink, mint-green and sky-blue, and tops the whole thing with a pattern of hundreds and thousands of sprinkles.

She adds, "You can't divide things up the way people say, for make-believe and for real, for work and leisure, for childhood and adult life . . . They all belong together."

A room in still life of Ingela's Ciao *fabric in red/black and green/black, with a yellow/black marzipan cake in the same Mickey Mouse polkadots.*

Ingela Håkansson in the family living room—something out of the ordinary.

38   *Cakes are called for more often than you think, Ingela maintains. Here are two absolute dreams in caramel-coloured cream, with lots of sprinkles.*

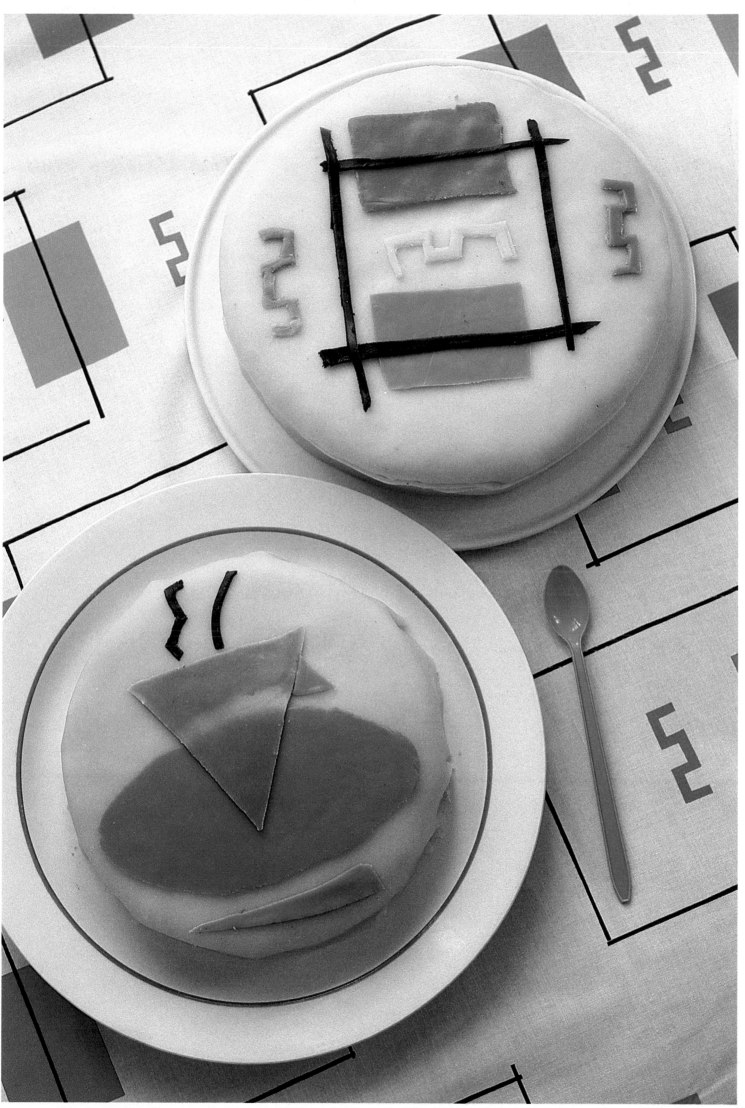

Two more cakes, this time with marzipan which Ingela has caramel-dyed and carefully fashioned to match her Arabesk and Kafferep fabric patterns.

39

ANNA ROOTH

An elderly Saami woman, talking about the decorations of the traditional Saami costume, once maintained that the further north you went in Sweden and Norway, and the more forbidding the natural scenery became, the more conspicuously the Saami made up for the austerity by the splendid coloring and imaginative design of their clothing.

Perhaps our need for beauty runs so deep that the sternest environment, the most austere circumstances, the most rigorous way of life can also generate flowers of the most delicate beauty, so that they spring up where they are most needed.

"And that's how it was," Anna confirmed. "People used to be so hard up that the villagers simply would not have had their traditional costumes if they hadn't done their own sewing."

So great was her longing for beauty that the flowers gleamed far and wide.

In the old days people vied with each other over who would wear the loveliest folk costume from the district, to show themselves in all their splendor on festive occasions, when attending church, at weddings, and at the major festivals. The luckiest were those who could make their own costumes, or had someone with that skill in the family; otherwise they had to buy their costumes—if they could afford them. Anna has sewn embroidered jackets for all her grandchildren, and had given them costumes for their confirmation. But since the Dala Floda Home Craft's Association supplies her with orders many years in advance, there are other fortunate people who possess a jacket sewn and embroidered by Anna.

She began her craft when she was 12 years old. A lady at Björbo taught her how to sew floral decorations for the local costume, using woollen yarn. Recently, Anna passed on her "stencils" of floral patterns to one of the two best embroiderers in Dala Floda—Anna Olsson, who is still active.

That is how these wool flowers travel!

Anna Rooth is wearing a påsöm *jacket and cap which she embroidered herself.*

Embroidered suspenders for the traditional Dala Floda man's costume. The woollen roses are embroidered on red cloth and the straps are of chamois, 1979.

Påsöm *jacket for the Dala Floda costume. The shirt, a double-breasted model with brass buttons, is sewn with red cloth with flowers of woollen yarn.*

BIRGER HAGLUND

SILVERSMITH AND GOLDSMITH

It's the simple things that are difficult: to simplify a form and still preserve the suppleness of its proportions, and give the overall composition an immediacy—this is something that takes a long time to learn, if ever. One man who has mastered it, in the craft of silverwork, is Birger Haglund.

Just look at his silver tub! Birger had intended to create an oval bowl. Gradually he "lifted" it from the base with a broad strip of silver that needed a narrow strip at the top for the sake of balance. Only then did he realize that it looked like an old washtub. A silver tub? Birger has traveled a long, idiosyncratic and highly decorative road to simplicity. He went from the foliage and fruit shapes of his 1940s Romanticism to his communion plate of the 1950s (Birger has supplied them to 35 Swedish churches), and then by way of his violent, heavily articulated forms of the 1960s, which came to an abrupt end in 1971 when Birger went to Afghanistan. He stayed there for two years, teaching 12 teenage boys from Kabul to work with silver and make jewelry.

"I felt that I had broken completely with my old way of working. These boys had never seen a silversmith's equipment before, and yet I only had to scratch a little on the surface to realize that primitive means *strength*. Here I met young people who express the many thousands of years' old traditions of their people perfectly naturally, as soon as they took hold of a pen. They were so incredibly charged with imagination, and the result was a kind of decoration I could never have dreamed of. It has nothing to do with perfection—it's the expression! We Europeans have gone so completely astray. My own production of jewelry, which had been bold enough here in Sweden, had to be put aside for a while in favor of silverworking, in which I was looking for a stronger meaning."

Today Birger produces functional objects, and sees no point in pure ornamental ones. He extracts from his customers a promise never to lock his creations in showcases but to use them. He would rather they dropped them on the floor and dented them and promises to repair them entirely free of charge, just so long as his items are used.

"Beer," he says, "tastes terrific from a silver goblet."

Bowl of silver, 30 × 25 cm, replica in the National Museum, Stockholm, 1984.

Overleaf: This entire "hoard" of silver was designed and created by Birger Haglund, mainly in the 1980s. Items include a large dish with a folded-over edge (1981), a cylindrical gilt vase (1978), candlesticks (1986), two engraved goblets (1982), sideplates (1984), and a small Tumbler for schnapps (1981).

Birger Haglund, silversmith, with two engraved Goblets made in 1983.

ERIK HILMER NORDÉN

DALA PAINTER

"The proper name is a 'Dala' painter (Dala as in Dalarna), not a Kurbits ('kürbis') or 'gourd' painter. It was the poet Karlfeldt who coined the name Kurbits, after the gourd that God prepared for a shadow over Jonah's head. But the plant withered and Jonah was angry. That was how everybody started talking about 'gourd' painting. I suppose it sounded classier."

Erik Hilmer Nordén is 82 years old and, he claims, in the prime of life. He sees retirement as a terrible punishment—why should you stop working when the only natural thing is to keep going as long as you can? Everyday Hilmer sits down to paint, and from time to time he teaches Dala painting courses at the Dala Floda Inn.

Many feel called to cater to the tourist trade's demand for picturesque "gourd" paintings, but few are worthy of the name "Dala" painter. Hilmer is a genuine Dala painter of the highest quality.

"In the 1750s and the 1760s, every Dala painter had his own style, or rather, he represented his own community and you could easily tell whether he came from Leksand or Rättvik.

Then, in the 19th century, everything became so standardized. A professional painter didn't have time for reflection—he just had to slap on the colors. You weren't an artist, you were a furniture painter. And for the most part they only did piecework. They had to complete a certain number of chests, coffers, or chairs every day; they were programmed, as it were, for a pattern. People were pleased when you came and pleased when you left—the painter didn't have any great social standing. It wasn't until the 1960s and 1970s that Dala painters were able to charge enough for their work, take more time, and call themselves artists.

"I was taught by an old Leksand painter called Urdin. I don't remember his Christian name; we just used Urdin. This was a 'flowering' course that I attended while working at the sawmill and later at the flour mill. Then I got a job painting in a woodworking shop. Painting on piece rates is the best training there is.

"I paint every day. You put different pieces together, using perhaps a classical situation and then filling in the empty space with gourds, sometimes adding words of explanation. If it turns out well you paint borders. The gourd is used as a filler."

Erik Hilmer Nordén.

Erik Hilmer Nordén painting in front of the Local History and Crafts Centre at Dala Floda.

Detail of Ålderstrappan ("The Ages of Man") painted in 1985.

The Dala painting Ålderstrappan ("The Ages of Man"). "In the old days, when the Dala painter was a poor craftsman, he painted straight onto wooden panels, flour sacks, tablecloths, and rags. In Rättvik you can see a painting where somebody has used the cloth from a man's shirt, and the seams of the sleeves are still there at the sides of the picture."

upp som ett blomster och faller, flyr bort som en skugge och blir intet.

år

60

70

80

90

SAM STIGSSON

WOODWORKER

"I suppose first and foremost I'm a bird-watcher, which I began doing since I was six years old. My aunt was a bird-watcher too. Once she showed me a cuckoo's egg in a nest and said, 'Let it be!' So I did."

Sam produces a kind of wooden "bird box" as he calls it, based on a classical model of a pencil box he saw at the Nordic Museum. It was only natural for a keen bird-watcher to turn the handle into a bird's head, and the designer in him just had to extend the tail section of the "box" to complete the picture. Sam has sold his bird boxes to the Hemslöjden craft shops, to the Swedish Society of Crafts and Design, and to the Design Centre. Sam Stigsson is currently working as a shoemaker — and as a bird-watcher, and woodcarver, and advertising consultant. Together these various occupations perhaps add up to that of "bird woodmaker," a term that seems to fit well enough when you first meet him.

"I've always lived in town during the winters, but when the bird-watching season begins in the spring I venture further out. In the summer I go bird-watching on the island of Gotland or in Skåne (in the south of Sweden). I work in a cobbler's shop, saving up to go bird-watching at other times of the year. I've been on bird-watching tours as well, to Nepal, India, Morocco, Greece, and France, and right now I'm making shoes so that Petter, my 10-year-old son, and I can go bird-watching in Kenya and Tanzania."

Sam finds the material for his bird boxes in demolition skips, and his patterns are based on sketches from his bird-watching forays. First he blocks out the shape with a saw, and adds the finishing touches with a knife before painting the box with water-based Allac colors. The head is then screwed onto the box.

"I only do Swedish birds which I really know well: gulls, terns, coots, mallards, tufted duck, pintails, oyster-catchers and shovelers. — I never make birds up! I'm a bird-watcher, so I only create from the real thing."

Sam Stigsson—bird-watcher, equipped with binoculars, sketch pad and notepad.

A skerry in the Dalarö Archipelago makes a good observation point for the ornithologist.

Among the bird boxes one can distinguish, for example, the gull, coot and oystercatcher.

Close-up of Oystercatcher *bird box, 1985.*

MADELEINE PYK

PAINTER

A lot of people dream that they can fly—that if they only hold their breath and push, they will take off and hover high above the ground. Without understanding why, one feels this is something very important; and this state is depicted in many of Madeleine Pyk's paintings.

Her figures can fly, walk the tightrope, turn slowly in a spiral around their everyday lives, their dreams and fantasies. All this is painted distinctly, simply, and with dignity: me and my bike, and Granny, and Babar the elephant, and the Katarina lift, and my glasses, and Kri, and Emile the cat. And the figures that are people and animals and shapes—they are there too. If you feel at home in Madeleine's pictures, then you simply walk straight into them. "We're flying . . ." ends one of the pages in one of her books.

"I collect images the whole time, but it's not easy—because things happen too quickly. I recently painted a picture called 'You Can't Keep Up with Yourself.' The reason why my figures hover, and walk the tightrope, is perhaps that you see things so much better from above. When I was young, I had top marks in physical education at school. I used to walk high up on the beam and climb ropes, and I wanted to be an acrobat. Three years ago I developed a fear of heights—perhaps as the years pass, one sinks further down. I'm really tired of these figures; they can strut around and get on with it as far as I'm concerned. Now I want to sit down and take things easy; I want to paint nature.

"Though there's no telling with me. I sit there saying all sorts of things that come into my head and I don't always know if I mean them . . . Out in the country the other week I saw a big tree with a tremendous red crown, which had been blown over by a storm, and I burst into tears. Dawn and dusk make me happy, and diving into water and seeing roe deer. It's not that easy to be happy in town. I go bathing early in the morning, and on my way I like walking along the street and seeing all the odd things and the people. Painting is difficult in town. I can try all day and then give up and put on my outdoor clothes to go for a walk instead, and then twilight comes and I sit there with my jacket and hat on, and I paint and I paint and I paint. If I take my outdoor clothes off and decide to do some painting, the spell is broken. Most of my pictures are painted that way.

"In simple terms, I've painted Slussen in Stockholm, where I've always lived, and my family—my private world. Now it's nature's turn.

"I've reached a stage where I would like to give everything away. One friend said that I was 'charged' and another said I was 'electric,' and I'd like to round off this period. When I was small I believed that talk made holes in the air and that if you went too fast you would actually tear the air. I think you get careful again as you grow older, and start longing for the incomprehensible grandeur of Nature."

Madeleine Pyk.

From Madeleine Pyk's sketch pad, 1986.

Slussen, *detail of painting, 1986.*

Grandmother, Babar and Alice, *1986.*

GUNILLA KROPP

POTTER

Gunilla Kropp has had many separate exhibitions and is one of the contemporary ceramic artists represented at the National Museum in Stockholm. After a period of working intensively with wrought iron on clay pots, she is now concentrating on black-glazed stoneware. But the greater part of her time is spent teaching.

"It seems impossible to make ends meet as a potter nowadays. Unless you have long production runs of fast-selling things, preferably something pale blue with lots of twiddly bits. But I've decided that I want to retain my self-respect, so I have to teach for a living. I have to take five or six courses, which occupies practically all my time. So many of the things that are worthwhile about the arts and crafts are going down the drain in modern society. But I insist on doing my best, and that gives me strength.

"I found that I have to use the nights to do what I really want. Then I sit utterly alone in my workshop, doing things that keep me alive, though I can't make a living from them."

To Gunilla, black-glazed pottery is a symbol of purity. Instead of competing with form, black heightens it. Black is primeval like clay, water, fire, and iron.

"In my workshop alone at night I do things just for the joy of it. I regard it as my mission in life to translate my happiness into shapes."

Black-glazed pot. Stoneware, 1985. A replica of this pot can be seen in the National Museum, Stockholm.

Overleaf: Pots with handles, lids, and bands of iron. Stoneware, 1975.

Gunilla Kropp with her black-glazed ceramic sphere. Stoneware, 1985.

ANNA AND MARJA CASPARSSON

EMBROIDERER AND PAINTER

Marja lives in her childhood home, a house known as Snäckan (the "Cockleshell") in Saltsjöbaden, with an interior that has remained practically untouched since the first half of this century, when the Casparsson family filled it with pottery, sculpture, and works of art, ceramics created by them and by others.

Most of Anna Casparsson's unique embroideries, the likes of which have never been seen in Sweden before or since, are still to be found here. And Marja painted Anna, year after year.

"She was my best model because she always sat still," Marja recalls. "She either played the piano or sat sewing. Anna said herself that she could never do anything by the rules, only for the pleasure of it. I had to learn the rules all right when I went to the Academy of Art, where I finished in 1928. I've only had one exhibition, at Konstnärshuset in 1936. I don't know if exhibiting was fun, because I never dared go there. But they wrote nice things about it, and I suppose they were kind. Anna didn't have her first exhibition until late in life, in 1945, when she was over 80, and she exhibited 50 embroideries. She died a few weeks before her hundredth birthday, and then I stopped painting portraits. Since then I've concentrated on landscapes.

"Anna told us four children a great deal about her own childhood, and she read to us a lot. She also wrote poetry and played the piano. Adding all that together, you get the same feeling as when you look at her embroideries. Our home was often full of contemporary artists, and Anna liked to sit with her needlework when we had company.

"Anna felt the need to be left alone, or to be appreciated by those around her in order to produce her embroideries and textile pictures; her imagination was beyond all the limits or conventions. Her technique was based on her materials, and the story she wanted to tell; she was never tied down by any preconceived notions as to the way an embroidery should look. A lot of her material was from theatrical costumes given to her by the actress Naima Wifstrand, and Anna took them apart and re-used them: brightly colored silken fabrics, lace, beads, spangles, and paste. Anna never made any sketches, she just started sewing in one corner and made up the story as she went along. In her embroideries, she described her childhood memories, told fairy tales and talked about her experiences.

"When we were small, Anna made dresses for me and my two sisters. I think we sensed that they were different, that we didn't look like the other children, and that wasn't always much fun. But we also sensed that she did the best she could. And that's always been good enough for me."

Portrait of Anna Casparsson, painted by her daughter Marja Casparsson.

Marja in her upstairs living room, where the philodendron twists and turns like a "tree of life" in a fairy tale. Paintings by Marja Casparsson, and textile embroideries by Anna Casparsson.

Interior from Marja's childhood home replete with Anna's embroideries and Marja's pictures, with the other collections of this art-loving family.

Memories from Sanary, *embroidered textile in the Casparsson home, Saltsjöbaden.*

Anna Casparsson's embroidered screen on a Biblical theme: "Expelled from Paradise."

BENGT JÄLLGÅRD AND INGVAR SAMUELSSON

SADDLERS

Saddlery is one of the endangered crafts in Sweden. Following a late but growing realization of the importance of crafts in contemporary society, efforts have been made in various quarters to protect the regrowth of various occupations. Bengt Jällgård and Ingvar Samuelsson, both of them traditionally trained saddlers, now have an apprentice who alternates between vocational school and working in their workshop—an arrangement by which both apprentice and master can make ends meet. As you admire Bengt's and Ingvar's work as journeymen and their masterpieces, you realize how many years it takes to learn the trade. Bengt's apprentice piece is an exquisite saddle of pigskin and suede. Ingvar's masterpiece is a frequently exhibited attaché case with an improbable interior that incorporates, in addition to the usual facilities, a small bar, with compartments for hip flasks, mugs, an ashtray, peanuts, and a radio, plus a small secret compartment.

"My grandfather was a saddler," says Bengt, "and the family indented me with a court saddler called Palmgren. I think I was a bit doubtful at first, but I grew into the trade and I've learned to love it."

"Same with me," says Ingvar. "Dad was a carpenter and I wanted to be a cook, but Dad talked to me like a Dutch uncle and fixed me up with an apprenticeship in the saddlery shop of the cooperative dairy organization instead. They had their own saddlery in those days, because the milk was delivered by horse and cart. So I had to sit there turning out one identical piece of work after another, in the old tradition. I think it's more fun nowadays when everything you do is a singular project and no two jobs are the same."

Today Bengt and Ingvar work with interior furnishings—paneling, tabletops, handrails, and bath fittings. The rest of their work consists of repairs and special orders. In the 1950s they made riding saddles for export to Cuba, and over the past ten years they have had a number of major orders from the Near East.

"The Queer East, right," says Ingvar. "Once we had this enormous job for the biggest luxury hotel in Baghdad, fitting out their nightclub. It was called 'The Thousand and One Nights', but three weeks there was enough for us. No place like home."

Bengt again: "The fact is that there are still people with money who long for beautiful, handmade things, and in our spare time we enjoy making things that we can keep for ourselves or give away as presents. Just once in a while I enjoy really going to town on a job."

Ingvar agrees. "Nothing beats the feeling of sticking your knife in the leather . . ."

Overleaf: Pigskin and suede saddle, by Bengt Jällgård, 1975.

Ingvar Samuelsson and Bengt Jällgård, Sadelmakarmästarna AB.

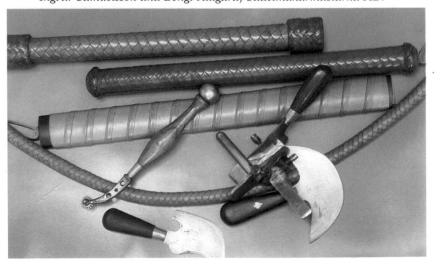

Supremely gracious tools, crescent-shaped knives (similar knives, of bronze, were excavated at Pompeii!), and specimen handrails, one braided and one spiraled with a bead.

Ingvar Samuelsson's masterpiece. An oxhide attaché case with luxury fittings which include a small bar, with spaces for hip flasks, mugs, an ashtray, peanuts, a light, a radio, and a secret compartment. Another model, made to order, has been sold to the Iraqi Embassy, to the King, and to assorted oil sheiks who consider themselves in need of an archive section, a writing case, and pocket calculator, a four-time-zone clock, a coded lock with an alarm device, and a bulletproof lining—all exquisitely upholstered inside with oxhide and suede. This version comes at about SEK 60,000 (1982).

ULLA HANNERZ

FASHION DESIGNER, TEXTILE SCULPTOR

In the winter of 1986, one of the Stockholm Cultural Centre's street-level display windows featured a party designed by Ulla Hannerz. A few dummies from the 1930s dressed up in modern skin-tight garments with snakeskin patterns and leopard print. The ladies' escorts were stuffed animals in human clothing—led by a coypu, dressed in Hell's Angels' gear. The window formed part of the exhibition "Homo Decorens."

Clothes are art, as art historian Broby-Johansen tells us. "Yes," says Ulla. "And there's a large amount of very bad art around."

Ulla Hannerz designs her own clothes for her own shop in the Old Town in Stockholm. VIC (Very Important Clothes) is regarded by many as one of the most amusing exhibition centers in Stockholm. She sells nothing but clothes of her own design: blouses, skirts, vests, dresses and the occasional coat. But there is more than just clothing in the big shop window. Ulla displays her garments on old shop window dummies with burlesque masks, and stuffed animals, with a fantasy which turns every window into a happening. Amusing and shocking, exciting and provocative—anything but ordinary. Ulla's own background includes a variety, such as designing ecclesiastical textiles and producing patterns for the fashion industry. Even as a child she knew that she was going to work with textiles. "I love fabrics; I dream fabrics. One dream is about what it feels like to walk into a big department store stacked with fabrics from floor to ceiling. A Treasure Island feeling of wanting just to wallow in the stuff. My mother has told me I was always like that, that I could stand there pinching the bolts to feel the quality of them, until the shop assistants were practically splitting their sides."

Ulla's textile sculptures give her an outlet for feelings of a completely different kind. "For long and faithful service" shows a tailor's dummy in a corset decorated with women's garters hung with brushes, scrubbing pails, babies, whisks, and saucepans. "Idi Amin's Ceremonial Uniform" is a khaki uniform covered all over in front with plastic medals of small human skeletons. "The Sausage Waistcoat" is made of slices of plastic salami assembled in the form of a waistcoat or vest, with hand-embroidered informative labeling: "Contains eyes, hooves, colorants and white specks of fat." This is a straight quotation from an authentic label.

In one exhibition catalogue, Ulla was presented as follows: "Ulla Hannerz' work emphasizes all that is softly feminine, but its charms conceal a tiger, a socially involved and critical person." She is a tiger with silky-soft fur and razor-sharp claws.

Pages 78—79: "Perfect," says Ulla. She is standing in front of the garbage, amid rust and scraped-off paint, yet in a light that is almost religious, with the cross of the garbage skip in the background. The observer feels torn between fury and laughter. "She" is Ulla Hannerz' textile sculpture For Long and Faithful Service, *1979.*

Shop-window dummy wearing Ulla Hannerz' red silk blouse. Ulla designs and makes up the prototype and calls in a cutter and a seamstress to produce the collection.

Ulla Hannerz and friends in her shop VIC, the unconventional surroundings of which perhaps can be said to reflect a lifestyle.

Overleaf: Silk dresses and blouses, designed by Ulla Hannerz.

JONAS BOHLIN

FURNITURE DESIGNER

Jonas Bohlin is the creator of a reinforced concrete and steel chair which has been much written about and debated. Is it ugly and uncomfortable, or attractive and creative? Post-Modernist or timeless? Or just simply trendy?

"The word trend is used wrong," says Jonas, "to imply that a trend only lasts for a moment. A trend is a long-term process of development in a particular direction. If my furniture seems disturbingly Modern, I suppose it's because it is so simple and uncluttered. Pure form is often highly expressive."

One hundred numbered copies of his concrete chair are in existence, one of which can be seen in the National Museum, Stockholm. Another is in the Roehss Museum of Arts and Crafts, and another in the ASF Gallery in New York. It is entitled "Concrete," and can be regarded as sculpture. In addition to being a qualified interior designer (a graduate of the National College of Art and Design), Jonas is a construction engineer (with four years' upper-secondary schooling to his credit) and fully familiar with heavy materials such as concrete and steel. "Concrete" was first made in 1980, using birch and steel. Later Jonas designed the "Zinc" bookshelf, also of solid birch, and standing on a concrete foot (for wall attachment) or horizontally, on a steel frame. He has also produced

another chair and a sofa. About five models is the sum total of his furniture output. How can you live on such a limited production?

"You can't. But I don't feel any compulsion to produce furniture, because I live on designing interiors. Anyway, nobody has asked me to produce more models. Perhaps my furniture will get more commercial in 25-years' time. At the moment it's being produced in short runs, which naturally makes it expensive. It's not that I'm in any way lacking ideas. I have so many I almost get fed up with them. And as for furniture shapes—they simply whizz past. So when a shape comes flying along, all I have to do is catch it and draw it. But then you have to turn it into a product, which is often difficult."

A man full of ideas, and not just on the subject of furniture and interior design. In 1986 Jonas helped to create Stockholm Mobile—a display center in the heart of that city for creative art and commerce, exhibitions and workshops, ballet and theater. Stockholm Mobile provides premises and supplies ideas. Jonas is also kept busy producing a periodical illustrating, in words and pictures, contemporary creative events in Stockholm.

Jonas Bohlin, furniture designer, with his Zinc, 1984, a concrete-footed bookshelf, and Concrete, 1980, a chair of tubular steel and solid birch, here painted blue.

KRISTIAN NILSSON

SILVERSMITH AND GOLDSMITH

Kristian Nilsson has attracted widespread attention in Sweden by his exhibition of fantastic jewelry. Some of his work was described in the following terms: "the buckle shears into the organic matter like a streak of lightning, creating tension" and "the movements of the waves toward the seashore turn, in this necklace, into a pearly foam."

His jewelry resembles no other new contemporary style. To find its "lineage" you have to travel a long way back in time, or perhaps to traditional folklore jewelry, where you find the same magnificence, the same powerful radiation and vitality.

"Yes, all right, but I think you have to learn to whisper instead of just shouting at the top of your voice," says Kristian, self-critically. "Simplicity is the next challenge—you have to have the same intensity in the simple as in the ornate, and I know of only one person who is a master at that sort of thing; there's only one Birger Haglund!"

Kristian himself trained as both silversmith and goldsmith, at the National College of Art and Design in Stockholm.

"I'm always working, but my entire life seems to consist of what other people call leisure—doing just what you want! I've found it suits me to live simply so as to have the time and financial freedom for my work. I don't have any of the things that other people *must* have: a car, a house, a weekend cottage. Decent clothes are my only vice, and then I don't care if I get water one day and champagne the next. I love contrasts. Hard work, followed by a great splurge and grand opera!"

Five or six pieces of jewelry a year are about what Kristian finds time to create. Most of them go to exhibitions, where they are bought by private individuals. The National Museum has also acquired some of his work as have his colleagues!

In the uptight climate of Sweden, Kristian may feel the odd man out, but this only makes him all the more determined to express himself with greater intensity than ever, to derive inspiration from his materials, metals, stones, and pearls, and from nature itself. At the moment he is dreaming about the sea and contemplating the possibility of going "fish-watching."

What torments him, by his own account, is being so critical, especially of himself. He is constantly spurred on by a frantic longing for grandiloquence.

Kristian Nilsson gazing into a piece of rock crystal.

The Finlandia necklace of Labradorite with a large silver buckle, designed and crafted by Kristian Nilsson, 1984.

Previous pages: The Hummerklo ("Lobster Claw") necklace, with aquamarines, corals, and oxidized silver in the claws, 1983.

The Copacabana *earrings of gold with yellow beryls, green tourmalines, rubies, brilliants, and amethysts, 1972.*

Guldkrabban ("The Golden Crab") with claws of gold and oxidized silver, aquamarines and corals, 1984.

EVERT LINDFORS

SCULPTOR

Evert Lindfors spends his winters in Lacoste, France, and his summers on the island of Djurö in Sweden. For most of the year, he produces a sculpture a day. He works, eats, sleeps, and works, modeling mostly in clay, sometimes casting in bronze.

"Time off? I can't take time off from living. I describe the present in my own way, I don't look for inspiration or good days. I have a feeling that tells me that my urge to narrate is, 'like a well full to the brim and overflowing.'"

Evert does not, perhaps, narrate in the classical sense; he is concerned to tell the story of things he knows about. One year he fashioned tools, another old clothing, shoes, and everyday objects which his neighbors had discarded or loaned him. He makes his sculptures tell us about the people who wore the clothes, about the sheer hard graft of the man who owned the coat or wore out the shoes.

"My imagination does the job of describing everyday work, everyday living, to my hands."

A critic once wrote that Lindfors was following in the footsteps of Van Gogh, or perhaps, indeed, in his worn-out cloth-ing, which he seems to have taken over and daubed with clay. When Evert Lindfors holds courses at the Artists' Collective Workshop in Göteborg, teaching his students about clay and sculpture, he is near collapse after only a few weeks. Neither he nor his students can stop when evening comes. Their imagination and creativity know no bounds, and Evert has to retreat to the solitude of Djurö to recover his strength. "But boy! You should see the stuff we turn out!"

There is no question of Evert buying clay. Clay is the gift of life, and you gather it yourself.

"Just as other people go picking flowers or wild strawberries," he says, "I dig my own clay and I test all the places I come to—ditches, meadows, streets that have been dug up in town. I clean the clay and dry it to the right consistency. Sometimes I add manganese to change the primary color, then I cut it and I fire it. Getting something that genuine out of life free of charge gives me this tremendous eagerness to do my very best in return."

Evert Lindfors.

Gym Shoes, *clay sculpture of high-fired clay from Skåne, next to the artist's own shoes, 1976.*

The Dress, *in progress in 1976, using clay from Provence.*

Bird, *made of clay from Kummelnäs, mixed with manganese to make the colors shift from iron red to dull brown, 1978.*

Flower, *made of the pure clay of the Luberon mountains. 1978.*
"This picture is truly nameless—flowers don't need names for each other, nor do birds, so I just say bird or flower because I experience their appearance namelessly."

SIGNE PERSSON-MELIN

GLASS DESIGNER

It is sometimes said that different countries have different design "vocabularies." Is there a modern Swedish design vocabulary, or have we let ourselves be unduly impressed by the international fashion of the time? There are clear signs at any rate that many designers are now feeling impelled to seek life giving roots of their own. But in many forms of art we have a number of special "mother figures," whose personal and articulate language of design has had roots of its own, roots that never failed. In glass and ceramic industrial design, for example, we have Signe Persson-Melin, an unmistakable piece of the jigsaw that is Swedish design.

After studying at the National College of Art and Design, Signe worked as a potter in her own studio until 1967, when she joined Boda Glassworks as an industrial designer.

"I'm not a glass blower; I'm a designer of industrial glass—these are two completely different crafts. I am both a potter and an industrial ceramics designer. There's a world of difference between sitting in your own workshop making the product, and sketching a design for the craftsman who will prepare it for mass production."

In 1971 Signe also began working with ovenproof glass, stoneware, cork, and cutlery for Boda Nova. In 1985 she became a Professor at the National College of Art and Design, taking over the glass and ceramics study programs. She feels that it is important for students to learn the elements of both

industrial design and free creativity. You never know which of them may later on prove useful.

"It took me a long time to learn to appreciate the role of the designer as much as the craftsman, pure and simple. Clay is solid and sensual, and you work with it for creativity as an artist. The designer has to consider the client's wishes, the production process, the financial side, and sales. As an industrial designer, it can be difficult to assert your own integrity; you are utterly dependent on efficient management. But the more you become involved with it, the more exciting it becomes. Things are difficult today, because nobody can afford to fail, but at the same time companies are discovering the importance of having their own unique design. It is the design as well as the price that decide whether or not the product will sell."

Signe has an aesthetical and economical way of also expressing herself in words. Urged to talk about Swedish glass that she particularly appreciates, she says: "there's something about our Scandinavian restraint that appeals to me."

Crystal goblet, made at Kosta in 1985. Originally made at Boda in 1975.

Pages 96—97: Boda Blom *and* Boda Oval, *both made in the 1970s.* Tulip Vases *from Kosta (1985) and* Kvadratburk *("Square Jar"), 1968.*

Signe Persson-Melin.

Parts of the Falstaff *service (1969), the* Sparkling *champagne glass (1975), and the* Ruben *chased beer glass (1966).*

Ruben *schnapps glass, 1966.*

EVA FÄNGE AND NILS MORITZ

MAKEUP ARTIST AND COSTUME DESIGNER

When a theater performance is successful, there is praise for the actors, the author, the director, and the stage designer. Less often do we read about the other important people who have worked on things like makeup, costumes, and lighting—things which have to blend successfully into the end result. In Molière's *L'École des Femmes* at Pistolteatern in Stockholm, the makeup and costumes play prominent roles. They are unconventional—and fun—with each actor resembling a mobile work of art. The structure of classical comedy, and the exaggerated decadence and elegance of the 17th century, are superbly captured in Nils Moritz' cheerfully bombastic costumes, made up entirely from used materials—everything from mops and dishcloths to curtains and bits of carpet—all full of color and humorously intensive. Eva Fänge has mixed elements of classical farce, clown makeup, and Japanese simplicity in this piece of bad taste.

Eva and Nils both freelance in film and the theatre. Eva's choice of occupation was not only inspired by great love of the theater. The one thing she really wanted to do was paint—and paint faces. After many years as a laborer, she discovered, more by coincidence, that there actually was an occupation where you could paint people's faces.

"I used to accost people who looked exciting and ask to paint them, but now I don't have to ask. I spent two years training as a makeup artist at the Dramatic Institute, and since then I have worked in that field for 13 years. I also teach at the Dramatic Institute from time to time. It is exciting, working with faces. I spend a lot of time at rehearsals seeing how the actors use their faces. Then I collaborate with each of them individually, trying to help them get to know their expressions and the possibilities offered by the reinforcement of theatrical makeup. We work on brush technique, and practice together."

To help the actors when they have to put on their own makeup, Eva prepares a schematic drawing, a photograph of a complete mask with a written specification of colors and the order in which they are to be applied.

Nils Moritz is now working more and more on stage design, although he is also an actor. He feels it is important to know as much as possible about the various elements that relate to a production. After one year at the National College of Art and Design, he went to sea and let real life provide the rest of his occupational training. Starting as an assistant in the Marionette Theatre workshop, he has worked his way toward the stage.

"Producing a costume is a very delicate operation—it affects the personality and expressive potential of the actor so much that things can get complicated. With stage design, you often have more artistic freedom. In *L'École des Femmes* I enjoyed myself, because the actors liked my sketches at once. The sketches were more like shapes, and the details came when they were sewn together. With our finances in the state they were, old left over fabric was just the thing, and the contrast with the lavish silks and brocades of the 17th century scored extra points."

Made-up mask for the part of Bélise in Pistolteatern's production of Molière's L'École des Femmes, *1984—85. The mask is superimposed on Kim Anderzon's face.*

Nils Moritz and Eva Fänge.

Mask/wig by Eva Fänge and costume/wig by Nils Moritz for Pistolteatern's production of Molière's L'École des Femmes, 1984—85.

Ariste—Björn Wallde—wearing a vegetable fiber wig, an oversize bow and ruffle of white felt, a narrow coat made from a bedspread, trousers with "padding" of surplus-store military blankets, and frills of bone-white felt.

Henriette—Annmari Kastrup—wearing a pleasantly decorated dress of a whole range of material, such as dishcloths, old curtains and bedspreads, partly dyed sky-blue.

Armande—Eva Thomé—is enchanting, in a dress made of similar materials, dyed rosebud pink.

ÅKE AXELSSON

FURNITURE DESIGNER AND INTERIOR DESIGNER

Art is expression—not appearance, and this is evident in Åke Axelsson's handmade chairs. This craftsman/designer builds his chairs after drawing a scale presentation of them. Åke, who spent four years in an apprentice school for cabinet-makers and another four years studying interior design, maintains that it is very largely the actual construction of the furniture that determines the design, not the other way around.

"That's how I see it, especially when you think about the original production process. I've tried to find out a bit about the history of furniture, but information about the way it was made is hard to come by. I found Egyptian and Greek furniture that interested me among lots of potential models from books and museums, and I've made full-scale reconstructions of some items. I've built a Greek chair from a vase illustration that clearly shows how the design grew out of the structural principle. The chair is more stoutly built where the greatest stresses occurred, and it has curved legs to give it greater stability. Long before the days of glue, joining techniques produced shapes of their own, with round slats and so on."

As an interior designer, Åke Axelsson has done a great deal of work in public places such as the Riksdag (Parliament) building, the Leksand Cultural Centre, and the Journalism House in Stockholm. These expensive settings seem a far cry from the field that interests him, that of everyday craftsmanship.

"My own craftsmanship mostly takes the form of one-off chairs, but I think it is important that we should have small-scale, craft-based furniture production in Sweden, which I have tried very hard to achieve. As a supplement to large-scale production, I've started manufacturing simple chairs in relatively short production runs, in close touch with the local market. There has been a manifest danger of the disappearance of craft-based furniture production. The threat was, and still remains, economic. But I believe that production can be adapted to circumstances—all you have to do is bring your furniture to people's attention. We *can* work with tradition, rational production and small-scale craftsmanship even today—and we must do it!"

Åke always returns to the chair as subject. Many of them hang on the ceiling of his own workshop, and they are stacked in every corner. The most exquisite chairs can be seen in his home, displayed in various groups, with no two chairs exactly alike. In one very private corner there is even a "lovechair" with two backrests.

Why chairs? "I see the chair as the most individualistic piece of furniture of all. Throughout the ages it has been the one item of furniture that has offered the greatest opportunities for variety of form and artistic expression. It is practically a reflection of Man himself."

The Torbjörn chair of Swedish beech, with a seat of woven cords and a detachable linen cushion. Designed and crafted in 1978. Photographed in the Riksdag (Parliament) building.

Page 105: Collage of handmade chairs, reconstructed from ancient Egyptian and Greek models. Made in 1972—1984. Some of the models are elaborations of the originals.

Åke Axelsson, interior designer, in the conference room at the House of Journalists, which he furnished in 1985.

Åke Axelsson, cabinet-maker, in his studio/workshop in Vaxholm. The walls are decorated with prototypes and sketches for further processing in small-scale production.

GOCKEN JOBS

TEXTILE DESIGNER

Ever since 1944, Jobs Handtryck, a family business, has been producing fabrics hand-printed with Swedish flowers. The patterns have been designed by the Jobs sisters, Lisbet and Gocken, who started as potters, until supplies of glaze and raw material were cut off during World War II and they switched to textile printing.

Gocken recalls that her brother Peer began cutting out her first lino patterns during the war. Production truly began during the autumn of 1944, leading to their first exhibition in 1945, in collaboration with Astrid Sampe at the NK department store in Stockholm, entitled "When Beauty Came to Town."

"I've been making flowers for almost 50 years," Gocken says, "I suppose I have a floral imagination. Perhaps it's my memories from our childhood home—the Sexton's House—in Falun. I've tried berry and insect patterns from time to time, and I've even done checked fabrics, but always with a tiny flower in one of the squares. I think that to love unpretentious wild-flowers like this is something very Scandinavian, and my very first print, actually, was called 'Wild Flowers.'"

Gocken may have a "floral" imagination, but it doesn't include fantasy flowers. She considers herself a Realist and Romantic, and she works from depictive sketches that are simplified and carefully checked against the reference books to ensure their authenticity.

Gocken finds herself living more and more at one with nature. "Just now we've been having these lovely summer evenings again. I walk out at eleven or twelve at night, and enjoy my special hillside. It's wonderful to see the flowers resting, and the bees working away. And then we human beings come along and take their food from them, but it's impossible to crush their energy and vitality; they make do with sugar solution and go right on working."

One of the first patterns Gocken Jobs made is called Rose and Lily.

Gocken Jobs among her flowers.

Detail of hand-printed pattern, Fru Lusta and Her Children.

JAN WILSGAARD

INDUSTRIAL DESIGNER

Jan Wilsgaard is head designer at Volvo's Product Design Department, which produces the designs for passenger cars, trucks, tractors, contractor's plants, buses, etc. The Volvo Design Centre, which has been called the heart of Volvo, has about 75 employees of different categories, including technical and artistic designers, pattern-makers and computer staff. As department manager Jan carries a great deal of the responsibility. although he would rather be doing design work himself, because the creative and artistic side of the job has a very special place in his heart.

"When there are too many meetings, and too much yakking, I go to Turin, where we have a model workshop where I can draw and make plaster models in peace and quiet. I enjoy working with my hands, and am convinced that a designer has to be both artist and craftsman."

Jan trained at the Göteborg College of Applied Arts as a sculptor and interior designer, worked with Volvo for 14 years, and then traveled to the Los Angeles Art Center on a scholarship to study transport design.

"These various study programs were a good combination. They trained me in sketching technique and in the three-dimensional vision that a sculptor requires. Our models are first sketched and then (here in Sweden) prepared in clay, in various sizes up to full-scale models, which are painted and then assessed in natural outdoor surroundings. For many years I did the clay modeling myself, and that's when I learned that even a slight adjustment can make a dramatic difference to the overall impression. As an industrial designer you must get back to the craft every now and then, otherwise theory gets the upper hand.

"Car design is very complicated nowadays; there are so many problems that have to be solved—factors related to production, the environment, costs, weight and noise, the laws and regulations that apply in different countries and so on—so that if it weren't for the stimulus of the challenge, the seriousness of it all would get you down. So many people's work is involved and there's so much money at stake that it takes a great deal of courage to alter the end product if you're not satisfied. I do that, if necessary, and I never give up until I am satisfied. Some people must find me pretty difficult at times. In this industry, a single person's ideas can be put into production by thousands of other people. They can cost billions of kronor and perhaps take five or six years to evolve. And in spite of all the computer hardware and software, the buck still has to stop somewhere.

"It becomes a bit of a strain sometimes, but there's never a dull moment; you do a lot of traveling and you get to know people and places all over the world.

"I get just as much pleasure out of chewing on a bone as dining by candlelight. When I was small, during the war, my family were refugees, and in the 1940s they rented a tiny shack in Porjus—two rooms and an outdoor loo, and that winter it was 52° below zero. When you have an eventful childhood, you often grow up pretty tough."

Jan Wilsgaard, designer, pictured here with a "passenger-car study," the beginnings of a clay 2.5-scale model which might develop into a new Volvo. Two sorts of clay are used, a hard modeling clay developed by the company and a softer international type. The modeling clay is oil-based and melts when heated. Models are also made of plaster of Paris, fiberglass, wood or cellular plastic and afterward painted. On the floor is a small fibreglass model of Jan's first car—a Volvo Amazon, 1953.

Jan Wilsgaard calls this car "a futuristic fiberglass rhapsody in form." Model for a preparatory development meeting.

GRETA AND AXEL PALMKVIST

STRAW CRAFTERS

Greta and Axel are a married couple living at Sunnanäng, a beautiful spot just a stone's throw away from Lake Siljan in Dalarna. Axel is a retired painter, and Greta a full-time housewife. Both have intermittently worked with straw. "It just happened that way," says Greta. "In the old days nearly every farm would make its own straw goat figures and candle holders.

"In the 1930s I made a few small goats to decorate the kitchen," she recalls. "We had a lodger then. When he saw them he thought I was talented, so he told me to keep it up. There was plenty of straw on the farm, of course, so it didn't cost anything. Then I went on to bigger things, like big goats, and I had to ask Axel to make me a wooden frame."

"It was just a hobby," says Axel, "but it turned out something more. I mean, you had to sow the rye yourself and then harvest it by hand with a scythe, drive it home and put it out to dry. After all, you can't go buying sheaves at SEK 25 a throw. Then you flail the rye, tie up the sheaves and put them to dry. Then you get out a bit at a time to work with, you remove the ears and leaves, you pour on a bit of hot water and leave it to soak for a while in the bath, and after that it's perfectly easy to work with. I think we get about 150 to 170 sheaves a year."

Greta and Axel only work to order, and they have more than enough to do. Anybody wanting a Christmas goat—a traditional decoration in Swedish homes—may have to wait up to six months. The couple produce all the old designs like big straw chandeliers, Christmas goats, advent candlesticks, and Christmas pigs.

Sometimes, when the local history society has an open day, they show the schoolchildren how to use a flail, and some of those interested have been taught the craft by them, though they don't know of anyone who has become a craftsman. The reason—as usual—is that it simply doesn't pay.

"It takes time and patience," says Greta. "We have the time because we don't watch television, and we work purely for our own pleasure."

Christmas goats—"the way they looked when we were small"—come in three sizes. The big ones are 75 cm high, with horns measuring almost a meter. Often they wear beautiful red silk ribbons around the stomach and muzzle.

Overleaf: The straw chandelier is a more recent model, built on a straw-woven base, machine-knitted onto a sheet of cardboard. The straw is woven upwards in eight braids, decorated with ears of rye. The candle is made of beeswax.

Greta and Axel Palmkvist both work at home on their crafts, using rye grown on the farm.

TORSTEN RENQVIST

To write in simple terms about a multifaceted and complex person as Torsten Renqvist is difficult, if not impossible. Looking at his work one must either try to understand the way it was created, thus enriching your personal experience with the analysis, or else ignore the method and go directly to the art.

Torsten says there is quite a difference between words and pictures, and he cannot escape either.

"I'm not a pure artist . . . Sometimes I'm jealous of the people who are: Cézanne, for example. At one time I wanted to be a writer and I still cart around with me a whole load of literary material. I can't sculpt without making it clear to myself, in a purely intellectual sense, what I'm about to do and why. Anybody encountering one of my sculptures and getting a direct real experience confirms what I want naturally—namely that, once they are finished, my sculptures should manage without me."

After 20 years as a painter and graphic artist, Torsten Renqvist began sculpting in 1967, first in metal and later in wood. He gets his timber from nature herself, using mostly aspen, poplar, and pine, but he also casts in bronze, concrete, and stoneware. His work, consisting mostly of sculptures for public environments and exhibitions, is on display throughout the world, and a book has been written about him. However, Torsten is a very private person, who likes to ski alone at Saltsjö-Boo during the winter, and spends a great deal of the summer, again alone, in his studio at Överkalix just south of the Arctic Circle.

"I've gradually come to realize that I'm not sensual enough to be a painter. I'm far too rational and realistic. It's easier in sculpting not to disrupt the wholeness of my carefully worked-out constructions, which are created piece by piece, adding shape to shape to make up the sum total. I start with a small model created in wood."

His most important tool is his knife—a small Mora whittling knife that is always swinging from his belt. Sometimes, at airports, he has been stopped in customs and required to "disarm."

"I get a bit red-faced," he says, "but when I explain that I'm a wood-carver, they're always pretty understanding."

A couple of his most cherished childhood memories are also connected with wood. "One is a beautiful fence that I saw before I was seven years old which I still think about today. The other is a pile of tarred railroad ties where I used to sit in the spring when I was a little boy, loving the smell of it and feeling on top of the world."

Fågel Fenix, one of the animals from the sculpture entitled Noah's Ark. Bronze cast from the wooden sculpture—originally carved in "jelly-colored" wood, 1976.

Torsten Renqvist outside his studio in Saltsjö-Boo.

The Shadows, *bronze sculpture on iron base. Here the original was a photograph of four girls who had jumped into the water on a summer's day. Torsten began by making a sculpture of the girls and then another sculpture of the shadows cast by the first . . . Like a carillon or an Aeolian harp, 1980.*

Wood sketch in poplar bark for Lautrec's Girls. *Originally a photograph of Toulouse Lautrec's models. 1982.*

SIRI SÖGER

In in a nationwide knitting contest in Sweden in 1986, the first prize was awarded to a very special and unconventional pullover. The style was plain enough, as were the technique and colors: the remarkable thing was the pattern. Someone had depicted nature—the deep forests and trolls with trees growing out of their heads, birds and glimpses of female figures with long hair—in a rhythm of mystique and fairy tale. I wanted to meet this knitter. On the drive to Gamleby, I could not help smiling at my high expectations of Siri Söger, someone of whom I knew nothing. But anyone who could knit a pullover like that, I felt, ought to be living in solitude in a cottage by the forest. No ordinary forest, of course, but a magic forest with huge, moss-grown erratics and wild animals everywhere. The knitter herself would be fluttering around among the logs and stones, wearing a long skirt, with hair cascading down to her waist.

That is exactly how it was.

Siri recalls: "My parents brought me to Sweden (when I was five) from Denmark, where I was born. There was something about the Swedish forest which affected me so powerfully that, afterwards, I never stopped telling everybody that I would be moving to Sweden one day. In Denmark I lived just outside Copenhagen, where there weren't any forests. So my forest was the magic one of Sweden. Four years ago, at last, I was able to move here and before long I'm going to be a real Swede—citizenship and all the rest. I have to live close to a big forest, unspoiled nature exercises such terrific power over me.

"I'm a pictorial artist which means that I weave pictures. I don't regard knitting as art. I knit to order, in order to make a living. When I start on a pullover, I start drawing on squared pattern paper. I switch off my intellect and let my hand do the work. Gradually I try to develop what my hand is doing, slowly, as if meditating. I don't plan what I'm going to do; I enter into myself and let things happen. Afterward, when I see the whole picture, I try to understand it. This particular pullover that won the prize turned out like a fairy tale, and it's called 'Once upon a Time' . . . My technique actually isn't all that good—just ordinary pattern knitting on round needles. I knit all-in-one and cut openings for the neck and sleeves.

"It took me a long time to get to the forests. I had to go the long way around with matriculation and a Danish degree in dairy engineering. But that reality belonged to my surroundings, not to me personally. Now I live in my own reality, alone and a long way from my neighbors. I live in my little house with no telephone, no radio, no television, where I've made all my own furniture. I fetch water and chop wood. I make clothing and shoes, and I grow some food for my own needs. I want to have a life of my own and I need concentration and solitude to find my pictures."

Siri Söger in the magic forest outside her house near Gamleby.

Front and back of the pullover Once Upon a Time . . . *The material is pure wool, 1985.*

The Castle, *pullover in pure wool, 1984.*

The City, *pullover in pure wool, 1985.*

ULF HANSES

INDUSTRIAL DESIGNER

Ulf Hanses' "Streamliner"—the glossily painted wooden toy car—is sold both to adult aesthetes and for young children to play with. *Form* magazine awarded it a prize and it is included in Playsam's export drive for educational play materials for pre-schools and other institutions.

"Streamliner" is perhaps the new Dala horse. Its creator was born and bred in Dalarna, and believes this has left an unmistakable stamp on his artistic vocabulary: in his toys and household products, and even in his new dental equipment!

"I think Dalarna design—with its rustic, articulate qualities—is in my bones. I can't stand 'chic', though I suppose even I have taken the odd sidelong glance at Italian design in the past. Today, though, I'm a functionalist. The longer you keep at it, the more you try to simplify your language. I think there's a simple reason why I've made so many toys. I grew up in a café. My dad was a baker and my mum ran the café, and nobody had time to play with me. So I built things with Meccano. Today I've returned to my childhood, creating toys that I wish I'd had. Now that I have children myself, I can bring a new model home and put it down on the kitchen floor . . ."

Can being an industrial designer create a conflict between the artistic and the commercial, when the two have to work together?

Ulf's view is that it is only natural for a good cake to have several ingredients. He finds it stimulating that the job should include elements of both solitary work and teamwork, artistic creativity and practical model-building, and how you structure the working methods depends on your personality.

"I've developed a technique that works well. When I get an assignment I just absorb it into my body, listening and asking questions. Then I do the rough sketch, playing with the job. Then, one day, the maturation process, half unconscious, half conscious, has taken place and I draw the model. Then I go to one of my two model-builders and we construct a complete replica *before* I show it to the client. That's usually a very effective approach."

Ulf Hanses sees a challenge in trying to put soul into mass-produced articles.

"The most pleasurable thing I know is to sit down every morning in front of an empty sheet of sketching paper."

Ulf Hanses.

Streamliner, in its developed form complete with driver and passenger. The car is made of bright-varnished solid beech and comes in several color combinations.

Streamliner, *Ulf Hanses' toy car for Playsam, was awarded* Form *magazine's honorable mention for Outstanding Swedish Design, with the following citation: "An object pleasing to both hand and eye, attractive to children and adults alike."*

Plastic button with sewing needle and prototype ABS-plastic thermos with rotating spout. Designed for Boda Nova.

125

INGER GOTTFRIDSSON

KNITTER

In the heart of the medieval town of Visby on the island of Gotland, there is a lovely old warehouse facing the alley known as Ryska Gränd ("Russian Lane"). Today it is a modernized house with wonderful roof beams, deep windows and wide floorboards. This is where you will find Inger Gottfridsson, who was born and raised on the island. Like other girls, she was taught to knit when she was small, starting with dolls' clothes and then, as she grew a little older, proceeding to such necessary articles as socks and gloves.

She does not regard herself as an artist. "My sister-in-law Ingrid and I had a very simple reason for compiling a book about Gotland knitting patterns: we couldn't find one. All we found was a very old collection of knitting patterns that was no longer on sale. We took some patterns from that book, and we traveled around the island looking for more; then we made up all the glove patterns as fast as we could. It was very exciting, but it still made me realize that I didn't want to knit commercially.

"I've always been a compulsive knitter, and I want to stay that way. If I have to knit, and things are demanded of me and I have a deadline, that takes all the fun out of it. So I work in an office instead! If my drawers and boxes start to overflow, I may put up a stall in the market and sell some of my work, just for the fun of it."

Inger appreciates simple patterns—a stripe, a flower—and she often uses the traditional pattern picture as a starting point which she simplifies and articulates in her creations. She vegetable-dyes her yarns and leaves them hanging from the roof beams or brightening various corners of the house. She showed me a boxful of the loveliest small dolls' mittens I ever saw; miniature mittens, beautifully made pairs with tiny, tiny thumbs. Another box holds baby socks, small works of art, made for the sheer fun.

Inger Gottfridsson is a natural custodian of tradition. She learned the craft from her mother when she was young, as a game that could become useful. She continued in adult life, making such additions and alterations as seemed natural, and she has now shown her own children how to knit, and what fun it can be. Her daughter's dolls have exquisite gloves, too.

Baby socks, with parts of the traditional Gotland Rose Pattern.

Overleaf: A random handful of the dolls' gloves found in Inger Gottfridsson's drawers. The patterns are "a little fragment taken from" the knitting tradition of Gotland, but the stripes and colors are Inger's own.

Inger Gottfridsson in the warehouse in "Russian Lane," Visby.

Teacups and coffee cups for the Gustavsberg Works. Stoneware, bone china, and flintware. Designed by Karin Björquist 1955—1985.

KARL-AXEL PEHRSON

ENTOMOLOGIST, PAINTER

In Karl-Axel Pehrson's home, the door between the reality inside and the reality outside is permanently open. All you have to do is walk in. Here are the beautiful cases of real beetles, shimmering, exquisite pieces of natural reality. In Karl-Axel's painted beetles, the original species are almost imperceptibly transformed and another reality presented. He has invented species of his own. With great seriousness and precision he transforms what we "know" into what we don't know.

Karl-Axel Pehrson has one of the world's finest privately owned collections of beetles, which he says have meant a very great deal to his "natural-lyrical fantasy painting."

"It makes me extremely bitter to think how the earth's environments are being destroyed. A lot of wood-living beetles need unspoiled forest in order to survive, and I can already show you any number of beetles in my collection that no longer exist. So there's a great deal of protest in what I paint. I paint the pristine, to underscore people's longing for what is unspoiled."

Karl-Axel started collecting Swedish insects as long ago as 1945. In 1955 he felt he had to go a step further, so he started on tropical insects.

"They affected my sense of color, shape, structure, and pattern. Their cilia, the overall impression of still greater fanta-

sies, nurtured a process which, above all perhaps, took place in my subconscious. I traveled quite a lot myself, but I actually obtained most of my beetles by advertising in local papers in the tropics, in New Guinea, the Philippines, and Fiji. I've had dealings with international beetle dealers, numerous missionaries, and I subscribe to a German magazine which runs an international pricelist. Prices are impossible these days.

"I've come close to beetles by thinking myself into their environment. The way they live in hollow tree stumps, loose sections of wood, or inside the most marvelous flowers. My imagination, my feelings, and my subconscious go on journeys. My sense of order and technical-mindedness are just instruments—it's the subconscious that does the work. I don't really give it all that much thought."

Karl-Axel Pehrson is represented in numerous Swedish museums and public places, such as the Gärdet underground station in Stockholm and Sturup Airport.

A box of Cetoniinae *(golden beetles), collected by Karl-Axel Pehrson.*

Overleaf: Fantasy Beetles, *various families, painted on Öland stone.*

Karl-Axel Pehrson.

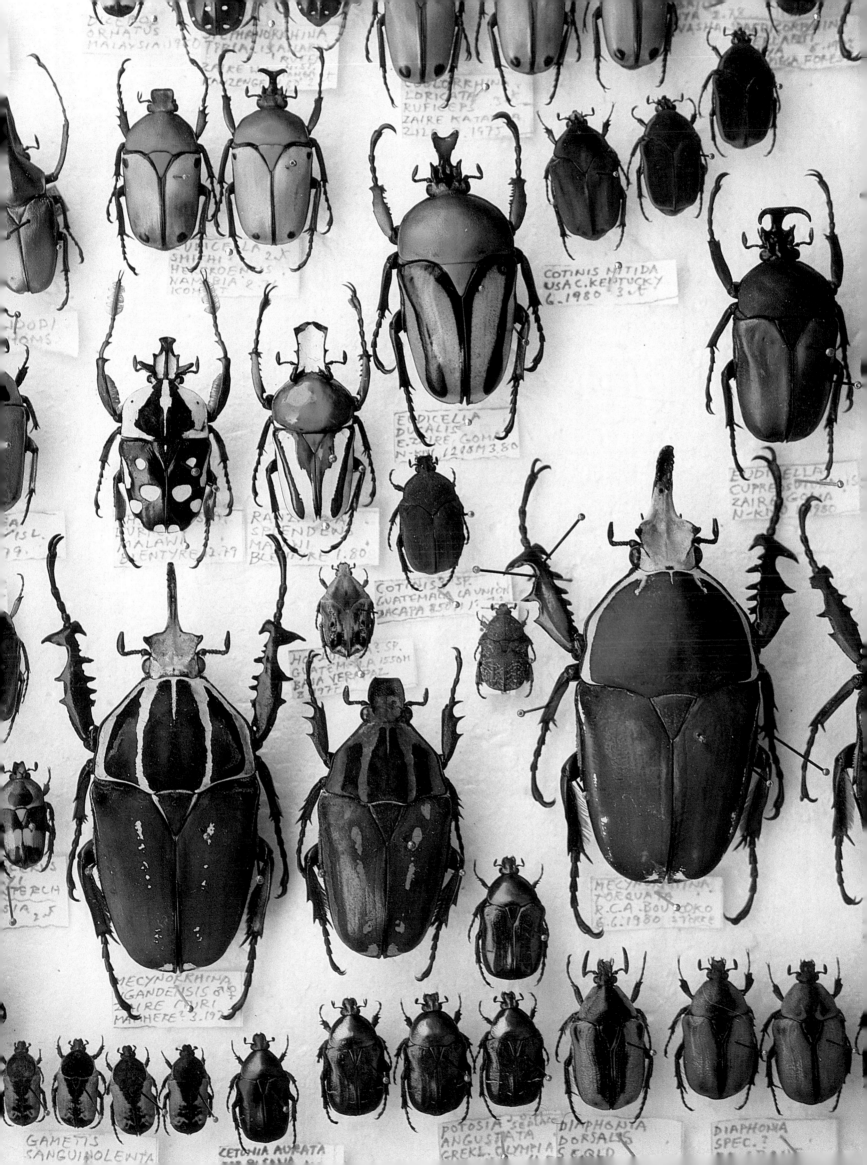

GRYTNÄS ERIK ERIKSSON

WOODWORKER

For a woodworker, preparing the wood is most important. To dry properly, all wood should be stacked with the bark downward, so that the water can evaporate.

"That's right. I had quite an argument with a neighbor once when we were talking about this and I had to prove to him that the bark had to be facing downward. That was the sort of thing you learned in the old days. I began working with wood when I was 14. Then I went to an auction and bought a carpenter's bench for 38 kronor, without having any money. So I went home to tell father what I'd done. 'Well, then, you'd better take the horse and fetch it,' he said, and he gave me the money."

Grytnäs Erik Eriksson has a farm near Leksand in Dalarna. Instead of livestock, the cow shed houses a big carpentry shop where he makes torches from dry sprucewood. Both craft shops and private individuals are anxious to buy his creations from wood shavings, which look rather like a hybrid between a Maypole and a gourd flower.

"Before electricity came to Dalarna, people used to make wooden torches for indoor and outdoor lighting, which burn brightly and last for a long time. You split old pinewood—preferably the sort you get from a stump with a lot of pitchy-colored bits—and then you bind them together into bundles. Another source of light, known as a *karbonist*, is made from the dried trunk of a young pine tree, with wedges driven in to make long slits that will let in the air.

"When using a torch or *karbonist* indoors, you had to remember the risk of fire, so you kept a bucket or tub of sand and water handy, and put the torch in a special holder. The smoke you just had to put up with. Dry spruce also makes firelighters or thick matches, which burn like the blazes.

"Dry spruce has practically vanished today because of the devastation of forests. When a tree dies naturally, you mustn't uproot the stump the way people do now. During the war, we put the stumps to use. People went into the forests, blasted the stumps to pieces, and burned them in charcoal furnaces. This gave tar and turpentine by the barrel, which was distilled, purified, and used as motor fuel. If you are lucky enough today to find a really good, old tree stump that has stayed damp, you can break it, split it, and dig out the roots with a spade."

Watching Grytnäs Erik splitting his wooden torches and whittling sticks, it looks very simple. The axe slides into the stump, which is rolled into position on edge; the pinewood splits exactly where it should and the sticks curl up before the knife in pure affection. He gives us a few hints about wood and heat:

The axe must be razor-sharp.

Pine and birch have to be split from the top down. Spruce has to be split from the root, to avoid tendons.

The best heat is obtained from birch, which has to be chopped quickly and not left lying around.

Pine, alder, oak, and mountain ash burn well, while aspen produces very little heat.

Spruce is not good in an open fire, because it can send sparks right across a room.

Wood should be brought in for storage in good weather.

An oven fire can be built and stacked from the inside, and lit with a piece of kindling in front of the wood. The same is true for an open fire.

An ordinary woodstove is filled with a pile of wood, and lit from underneath with a piece of kindling.

Grytnäs Erik Eriksson.

Traditional break-off fire lighters made from old dry spruce.

139

Grytnäs Erik in the woodshed, demonstrating how to split wooden torches.

The crafts shops are selling fire lighters as Christmas decorations.

A dry spruce, and the knife cutting the fire lighters into shape.

A razor-sharp axe splits dry spruce into torchwood.

A karbonist, long splinters of dry spruce. In the old days, flares like these were used both indoors and outdoors.

MARGUERITE WALFRIDSON

DRAFTSWOMAN, INDUSTRIAL DESIGNER

Some people very clearly draw their nourishment from nature. Marguerite draws plants, grows plants, dries plants, eats plants, and writes books about plants when she is not teaching about plants or taking photographs of them. In the meantime she talks about plants. Or she fights for their continuing life, which she sees as fighting for her own life.

"The biggest threat to humanity is our own lack of understanding and respect for plants. Once we have destroyed the conditions for plant life, there will no longer be any oxygen. And then we won't be capable of existing either. Plants are not cosy little things that we can have or do without, they are the necessary condition of human life.

"Sometimes I fight tooth and nail to get people to understand what we are letting our politicians do when they clear the forests, put down asphalt, spray pesticides, and so on. Knowledge gives you strength and enables you to put up a greater resistance."

Needless to say, it is plants that give Marguerite her fighting spirit. "Plants have beauty, fragrance, and flavor which you can play on just like music. I compose with, say, the help of a cabbage and a few sprigs of fresh thyme, and the result is so splendid I can just sit there laughing. I make a blossoming salad out of flowers, sprigs of herb, and a few drops of almond oil, and everyone around the dining table feels happy. In Gotland, where I spend the summer, I have a real kitchen garden, and then I load the car right up with dried plants for the winter in Stockholm. I want to tell people about everything we get for free. About how simple it is for us to make our lives richer. You can grow things on your balcony and enjoy life in the smallest of kitchens. In Sweden, of course, we can pick flowers from the hedgerows and fields. Everything is just handed to us—look at the incredible beauty of what we call weeds!"

Marguerite Walfridson is concerned to help bring about a revival of the forgotten, rejected knowledge we once possessed about our plants, adding to it a knowledge of species in other countries that can also be cultivated in Sweden. Perhaps what she likes best of all is to draw wild plants. "Once upon a time plants gave us food, medicine, heat, building materials and clothing—and it's worth reminding people of that."

Marguerite in a Gotland meadow, with an armful of wildflowers.

"Flowering lettuce"—a composition of beautiful lettuce leaves and various exotic fruits which taste as good as they look—topped of with a few fragrant drops of almond oil.

Marguerite puts the morning's harvest of wildflowers in an old stone jar. Some of them are hung to dry, after which they will brighten up the home all winter.

Drawing, Garden Bouquet, 1985.

JACK SANGWILL

INTERIOR DESIGNER, CABINET-MAKER

In Kocksgatan, Stockholm, lives an interior designer, in a very expressively furnished and decorated apartment. Jack Sangwill receives me in his home, to show me *The Home Hearth*.

"*The Home Hearth* looks like an open fireplace, but it is a cocktail cabinet I've built. You open it from the top with a handle which is a rainbow trout's tail, and the bottom part serves as an ordinary cupboard. It's made in rough-sawn pine which I have painted in oils, and the entire mantelshelf is marbled."

Next to *The Home Hearth* stands *The Armchair*, which is large and generous, made entirely of rough-sawn, thin pine — and is extremely comfortable to sit in!

"It was my graduation project at the National College of Art and Design in 1980. I made the whole thing myself, from sawing the length of pine from the log with a bandsaw to designing it and doing the actual carpentry work. It expresses the feeling I want to convey through furniture — that you have to be able to sense that it has been fashioned by hand. That radiates a kind of warmth which I think everyone can feel."

At a furniture exhibition where *The Armchair* was shown for a year, it attracted attention as contrast to the latest modern Italian design.

"When people saw *The Armchair* it made them happy, and I think furniture has to be fun. Personally, stylized environments bore me to death, and I often feel that people have a serious problem with interior design. Instead of something that makes them happy, it's something they acquire for the purpose of keeping up with other people. Everything has to match, with complete uniformity of color and style. I want to show people unconventional alternatives, perhaps furniture with a sense of humor and warmth. Anything home made deserves respect — as does our traditional peasant furniture."

Jack Sangwill also works as a painter, and he has yet a further speciality — marbling. His own bedroom and hall have marbled walls; the sitting-room table is of marbled pine with the thickest possible coat of car paint; and he marbles hotels, restaurants, and discos to order.

Table of marbled pine, the top thickly coated with car paint, 1983.

Jack Sangwill in his living room with his cabinet The Home Hearth, *1984, which opens with the tail of the rainbow trout, and* The Armchair, *1980, made of pine slats.*

RAINE NAVIN

SCULPTOR

As an artist, Raine Navin expresses himself both in concrete materials, such as papier-mâché and textiles, and in more abstract forms, for example when he works at getting other people to express themselves creatively, to share experiences, and to learn to "see" their own fantasies.

He has been a knitter ever since childhood, learning at an early age to knit everything his family needed—socks, gloves, and sweaters. One year he knitted a sweater with needles made from swan's feathers.

"I imagine things all the time," he explains. "For instance, that I'm living a long time ago and have to make do with what nature provides. Once I used sheep-wool yarn and two swan's-wing quills and knitted ten-centimetre lengths which I then sewed together to make a pullover—a 'swanover'. I love round balls of wool, all round shapes."

Primeval, simple materials and shapes make up Raine Navin's "symbols." Round shapes have fascinated him for years, and he has fashioned beautiful spheres using his own papier-mâché technique. Other round shapes became a hat of the same material: you admittedly can't wear it, but it's super to hold in your hands!

"I don't always plan what I'm doing. Things just turn out the way they do, and then afterward I understand why."

Raine does a lot of work in schools, traveling around with different projects, helping the children to decorate their school or stage special exhibitions. Children find the language of form easy to understand, and have enjoyed his knitted work in the form of "Oversocks for a Bicycle", "Winter Tyre", and "Oversocks for Skis". He also shows them a composition called "My Brother Is Dead". Raine tells them its story:

"When I was small I knitted a cardigan for my brother. When he died a few years ago, I unraveled it, and now I have five skeins of wool instead."

But Raine always reverts to the round shape. He thinks the reason he likes it best is because you can cup your hands around it.

Sphere *of papier-mâché, which consists of newspaper soaked in water and then shaped, 1984.*

Raine Navin with Hat *of papier-mâché, 1980.*

ELIN LINDGREN

KNITTER

There's still a lot of knitting being done in the farmhouses and homesteads of Gotland; not so much as there used to be, but enough for the family. Yet homemade gloves and socks are not easy to come by; the hourly pay for somebody selling them is about 3 kronor. Still, some people keep at it.

"Yes, because otherwise a single mitten would cost about 300 kronor, and that's not realistic," says Elin Lindgren, born at Endre, on the island of Gotland, which has been her home ever since. "It's better to use it. Now I've finished knitting for my own family. The girls have grown up and do their own knitting, but I find knitting pleasant and restful. I just use the old patterns; there are any number of them and I think they're very beautiful. It would be dreadful if the tradition of knitting were to disappear on Gotland."

Finding patterns was not easy for Elin, because women used to learn from each other and kept the descriptions in their heads; so as the tradition of knitting grew weaker, a good many of the old patterns disappeared. Finding old gloves to copy was practically impossible, for these reasons.

"I've done the same as my mother and grandma used to. First you knit the gloves, then they are used, and you wash them and darn them as long as you can. When they're completely worn out, you give them a final wash and sell the material to the woolshop, in part exchange for new wool. A piece of wool was never wasted. At least, that's what we used to do before the war, but then people got more wasteful, they began buying new things and throwing old things away. All I have left from the time my girls were small is just one pair of stockings. They were not worn because they were too prickly and you don't sell things that haven't been used, so they were kept lying around."

There are many stories from both Dalarna and Gotland about women knitting whenever they had a spare moment. The maid carrying the milk pail worked at a stocking as she went. The fishwife driving a horse and cart down to the beach to collect her husband would have the reins around her neck and knitting in her hand, and she would do the same when bringing in the hay. Elin Lindgren knits while she watches television. She gets most fun out of knitting "Björkume-Ole's skullcap," which is the subject of an allegedly true story.

"Björkume-Ole was only 97, but the children thought he looked at least 100. He would stand outdoors chopping firewood, looking ever so funny in his knitted skullcap with a tassle. The skullcap looked as old as Björkume-Ole himself, and the odds are that he had never taken it off, day or night, since first he put it on. Everyone felt that Björkume-Ole should have a new skullcap, just like the old one, nothing new-fangled, because both his father and grandfather before him had similar skullcaps. It was black-and-gray with a wheel pattern at the top and a tassle reaching down to his ears. It had to be knitted without a flaw, by an innocent child, so as to give the owner a long life. When the cap was knitted it was rejected because the swirls went counterclockwise, which meant that the wearer would never get to heaven . . ."

Just to be on the safe side, Elin always knits the swirls clockwise.

Detail of Elin's knitted cardigan in the traditional forget-me-not pattern from Tofta.

Elin Lindgren knits traditional Gotland patterns.

Gloves in traditional Gotland patterns. From the left: Hooks, with a pattern description from an elderly woman at Endre; Dalbo, pattern from a farm in the parish of När; Tendril, an old Endre pattern; Roses, from the parish of Rone; and Lingonberry Twigs, after a bridal stocking from the 1850s in Gammelgarn.

Björkume-Ole's skullcap, knitted with black-and-grey wool from young lambs, with a patterned border, a whorled top, and a tassle that hangs down to the ears.

THOMAS LUNDQVIST

PUPPET-MAKER, DRAFTSMAN

When the colorful blue and red Cirkus Abelli theater bus pulls up in the courtyard in front of the Ethnographic Museum in Stockholm, you know that the theater has arrived. The audience climb into the bus, sit down in front of a small stage, and watch and listen to a story of the battle between good and evil. The puppet-maker has also helped with the script, the stage design, and the music. His name is Thomas Lundqvist, and he insists that puppet theater is not really only for children.

"We produce plays about serious and comic events to which we can all relate. Life and death, love and evil, power, cunning and weakness—told in a way that both children and adults can understand, and the greatest part of it is experiencing something important together. The one person who expresses this tradition of visualizing things, though in his own particular and brilliant fashion, is my favorite: Chaplin. He's a real puppet!

"Otherwise the most sophisticated puppets are marionettes. My technique is based on Japanese *Bunraku*—a very simple form in which you hold the puppets and make them move in a sophisticated manner as you describe dramatic events in fairy-tale form."

Thomas originally planned to be a painter and studied at the Academy of Art. Together with 20 other enthusiasts he launched a big project entitled *Blomkraft* ("Flower Power"), putting on puppet dramas with music. Gradually he has experimentally evolved other types of performances with a great deal of puppetry and music. The very first impulse came when he saw an Indian dance drama group, *Katakali*, performing as puppets. The tradition of living puppetry still exists in the East, and has inspired Thomas and his friends to find subjects that will suit a Swedish audience. Puppetry also works very well on television, but in some places there is a strange lack of understanding for this kind of art.

The puppets Thomas makes are works of art with refinements such as movable eyes and fingers. His puppet Goliath is so ingeniously constructed that his head can be chopped off, but he can still, when necessary, re-appear as good as new.

"If we can't succeed here in Sweden, we'll take the bus and our families and go abroad. The language of puppetry is international."

Wooden puppet head made by Thomas Lundqvist "mainly to learn the technique," and prototypes of puppet arms, and hands which can be clenched and unclenched—one of them can even point its finger! 1977.

Thomas Lundqvist.

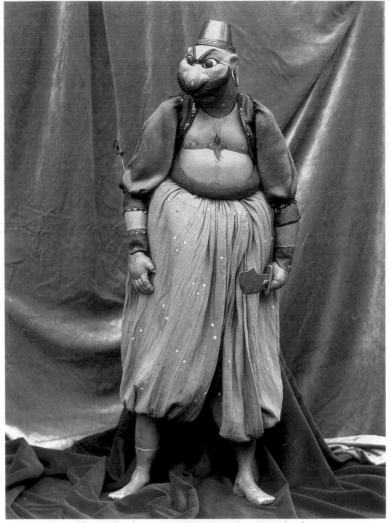

The Goliath puppet from David and Goliath.

Burlesque puppets made by Thomas Lundqvist for the Cirkus Va-
rieté show, from the "At the Dentist's" scene. Their names: Yodel,
Gyllensnusk *and Doctor Schwindelfritz. 1985.*

154

Thomas Lundqvist is a trained painter and makes all the posters for his puppetry productions.

ANNA WÅLSTEDT

WEAVER

"Wålstedts of Dala Floda" is a household name for people dealing with textiles. Today, the second and third generations of Wålstedts work in the textile factory, from which you can buy unique yarns that impart a sort of shimmering quality to woven fabrics and knitwear. Anna was a young girl when she joined Wålstedts as a weaver in the 1930s. In 1936 the son of the family, Lasse, who had just become her fiancé, opened a spinning mill, and they were married in 1938. Anna wove and managed the household, which in due course came to include four children and many trainees from the workshop.

"Nowadays I do more weaving than ever. I didn't have much time to spare for my own weaves when I had to show others what do to, and had other things to attend to. Everyone had to lend a hand, but that was the way things were done in those days. We were hard-working people, and we were tremendously happy in our work. My family had a small farm and all of us, young and old, used to go off to the fields with a picnic basket. We stayed together; we worked and we relaxed together. There's a special kind of pleasure about working within a family, and in my new family I was able to go on working that way. Although I've never known anything else, I do feel privileged. Sometimes I think that I would have liked to study when I was young, but my father—like other fathers in those days—didn't think it was worth paying for a girl's education because she would only get married anyway. I think I would have liked to have been a teacher. Still I've enjoyed myself. And I've never had to leave home and the children."

Anna's mother taught her to weave when she was only 12 years old. She began by entering (putting the warp thread through the heddle) and weaving simple patterns, and Rosepath, she says, is the weave she enjoys the most. She uses traditional techniques and feels that there is great freedom in varying the patterns and colors.

"You seldom get two weaves that look alike. Before I start I think about what I'm going to do; I look at my yarns and I pick out some nice colors. Sometimes I draw inspiration from attractive photographs of natural scenery, and then I just let the weave develop in the loom. I don't pretend to be an artist; I like working more in the quiet. My cloths, mats, and blankets are sold here, on the farm. Sometimes I make demonstration rugs, for example, to show what our yarns look like when they are finished."

The Wålstedts no longer keep their own sheep. They buy wool from the native Swedish breed in Dalarna, Värmland, Västmanland and Gästrikland. They sort, wash, dye, and spin the yarn, which is divided into four qualities: rug wool, tapestry wool, fine wool, and fur wool. These can be variously combined for use in everything from fairly coarse textiles to the finest babywear.

"Now I've reached an age when I want to make sure that something of what I've done will be passed on to the family. For Christmas last year I wove bed blankets for all our eleven grandchildren."

Anna Wålstedt on the porch of the family home at Hagen, Dala Floda.

Rosepath cloth, 180 × 70 cm, which normally decorates the drawing room table.

Twill coverlet, 155 × 230 cm, its colors inspired by a cloudberry swamp.

157

GUNILLA PONTÉN

FASHION DESIGNER

Gunilla Pontén is one of Sweden's best-known fashion designers, and innumerable articles in women's magazines have described this colorful, beautiful, and amusing woman. Her clothes are equally amusing, colorful, and beautiful. Gunilla is "historic" in the sense of having helped to create teenage fashions in the 1950s, when fashion was still divided into children's wear and ladies' wear. The teenage Gunilla walked up and down Kungsgatan, in the center of Stockholm, wearing homemade, cheerful, shocking clothes and holding an orange in one hand—for the sake of color! She matched the color of the orange with home-dyed orange shoes, which was enough to launch her own fashion career with a hurricane-strength wind in her sails.

"I'm a child of Fellini! I love it when people express themselves as *types*, when their characters are expressed by the way they look. The more distinct, the more wonderful. I'm utterly devoted to helping them do just this. I want to paint a person, a character, with my clothes. And I know that I can help a woman see for herself what type she is. Not the fashion flavor of the month—it goes deeper than that. Many women just long to be taken care of by somebody who can help them 'paint' their type into being. The hair on my neck stands on end when I get a chance to do this. I'm not talking about the banal, glamorous-type beauty. I'm simply not interested in all that. I want to work with character, with great gestures and dramatic shapes—and a dash of humor—that little touch of self-irony that suggests a distance from it all, that it really isn't that deadly serious. A suggestion of something contradictory, to balance the whole thing.

"My best clothes are a combination of different patterns and qualities. Often simple in form, and then they have that touch of humor—brilliant red laces, say, on black clothes, superfluous fishwives' mittens in a contrasting color, and preferably something outrageous on your head. The overall impression is important. People have this tremendous uncertainty about mixing and matching—that Swedish lack of courage, that you can see in people's clothes, needs me. I'm terrifyingly strong—you have to be, to keep going in the 'rag' business.

"Of course it occasionally gets me down, but I always pick up the pieces again. There are so many things in life that I get a kick out of: colors like lemon, orange, melon—they're so fruity they make your mouth water . . .

"A musician needs to play, an artist needs to paint—and I need to design clothing. It's that simple."

Gunilla's daughter Beata is wearing a knitted pullover. The pattern and design suggest some of the vigor and excitement of Gunilla Pontén's clothes. The material is alpaca/lambswool, with some artificial fiber and lurex. From her 1986 autumn collection.

"It's the small details that count, a touch of humor to show that clothes shouldn't be taken all that seriously . . ." Beata wearing a pillbox by Gunilla Pontén, in "art déco" fabric from her 1986 autumn collection, and a matching necklace made in collaboration with Lotta Hallin, who used beads, yarn, and scraps of cloth.

Gunilla Pontén.

Hugo Anderberg

POTTER

Hugo remembers exactly when he started work as a potter. It was on Saturday, 3 November 1925.

The reason he remembers it so exactly is perhaps that the day was so important to him, or perhaps because so many people have asked him. Hugo must be the best-known, still-active potter in Sweden today. A few other members of the old school are still around; but Hugo is not optimistic about the future.

"This type of potting is on the way out, but I don't let it worry me. I'll soon be dead, and then I won't give it a thought."

Hugo has been employed at various times, had his own workshop, and has now finally leased the Raus Stoneware Factory, just outside Helsingborg. For more than 50 years he cycled to work at the factory, but for the past 10 years or so he has used a moped, his legs not being what they used to be. The City of Helsingborg has bought the factory, which is now to be restored as a historic building.

"This is just a hobby now. I come here and work when I feel like it, and I only fire one kiln a year."

His wife Greta, his only assistant nowadays, takes up the story: "We two keep struggling on. Hugo can't have an apprentice, even if anyone wanted to learn the trade. There are no modern conveniences here, no toilet or lunchroom as there has to be according to law. So it's only the two of us who can take things as they are. I come in a few days each month and do what I can. Water the pots inside, put them to dry, and stack them to make room. Hugo still throws the four models on our pricelist: jam pots, jars, salt-glazed ware, and low pots. It's the jars that people use mostly. At home we use all the models, not as ornaments but for practical purposes. We have jars for butter, jam, and marmalade, our food is in bowls and the milk in jugs that Hugo has made. Even the youngsters around here have learned to pickle and salt things down—it's cheaper and nicer than the bought stuff. Salt-glazed ware doesn't absorb flavors and if you make your own food you always know what's in it."

Hugo Anderberg throws the classical Raus pots in the traditional way and his annual firing follows the traditional procedure exactly, using a coal-fired kiln and rock salt.

"This is an ancient craft and you have to do what is necessary. I suppose you can always do a bit of fancy stuff on the side, but it's the solid craftsmanship that counts."

Hugo Anderberg at his potter's wheel in the Raus Stoneware Factory, built 1911.

Inside the Raus Stoneware Factory, which produces saltglazed stoneware for everyday use. Old equipment, worn furniture and half-forgotten pots here and there add a distinctive charm. "My goodness, this place is dirty," says Hugo.

Pots made in 1986. The models are 6 and 15 litres, made of saltglazed stoneware of the traditional Raus model.

BO AHLSÉN AND HANS LINDSTRÖM

ARCHITECTURAL PAINTERS

The Ahlsén Group is concerned with giving both interiors and exteriors a whole new dimension. With their paintings, their planning and their décor in general, they can transform a room, enlarging or reducing it with the deceptively natural proportions of their painting, and creating entirely new perspectives to convey an extra experience of space.

Bo Ahlsén and Hans Lindström, two of the artists in the Ahlsén Group, which also includes architects, believe that every architectural painting should include a symbol; the painting must speak a simple, clear language, even while conveying mysticism and fantasy.

"When we paint some gigantic tree in what is really a rather sterile housing environment," says Hans, "it must not take the place of real trees. Our tree is one of the many parts of a sort of rehabilitation program to improve the environment, an environment that includes real trees."

As Bo puts it, "You can't suggest to people that they buy either books or a refrigerator. A painting can't take the place of a bathroom, but it can improve your life. Our job is not to liven up dingy surroundings, but to influence the whole pattern of things. We color and structure environments, both overall and down to the details, taking into consideration both the material and the cultural side. A link is needed between these two concepts, and we put a great deal of work into this."

Hans and Bo collaborate very closely on the actual painting. First they prepare a sketch, then they make a model of the interior or exterior. When the decoration starts, they can sit together on the same scaffold painting the façades.

"On occasion," says Hans, "we've started at the opposite ends of a painting and met in the middle. But sometimes we work separately, or else one of us begins and the other takes over. I think you have to have the same artistic chemistry."

The Ahlsén Group's clients range from national and local authorities, county councils and housing corporations to private individuals. The Group has decorated schools, hospitals, play facilities, suburban housing estates, and even the Royal Palace in Stockholm!

"We want to show the small space in the large, the large space in the small."

As part of the urban renewal of Botkyrka, the Ahlsén Group, together with Lars Sterner of the 5-ARK Group, produced a new color scheme. This painted tree on the wall of a multistory building provides a clear accent in the environment, creating a sense of space between the sterile structures. 1981.

The Ahlsén Group, here represented by Bo Ahlsén and Hans Lindström, sitting in their stage setting of perforated sheet aluminum shaped in the form of clouds and foliage. This artistic decoration, designed for an office building in Stockholm, was a joint project with architect Lars Ljunglöf, 1981.

ELIN VINGE

Not far away from Leksand lies the little village of Hagen. In Hagen there's a farmstead that is an absolute idyll, and in this idyllic farmstead lives Elin Vinge. The windows of the local houses are decorated with paintings or with the sewn lace known as sprang. At Elin's you can see the fragile sprang shimmering in the windowpanes, and inside the entire kitchen table is decorated with enough sprang for an exhibition. Net and sprang needlework is an old craft that is still kept alive in study circles and pensioners' clubs. Elin has always painted and woven. An eye operation forced her to change her creative habits, so she took a couple of courses in sprang.

"I've shown my things at a lot of exhibitions but I've never sold any. Because I don't want to. Sometimes I give things away, it's not a question of business. I don't mind it taking a long time, I have to keep myself occupied. First you make the net, which can take two days and has to be done with a special needle. Nowadays a lot of people simplify matters and crochet the net. You use hooks and a beater and semi-bleached linen yarn. For the actual embroidery you use a softer linen yarn and an ordinary needle, and you work with a darning stitch or sometimes with 'shingle', as we call it."

Elin Vinge cuts out knitting patterns and cross-stitch patterns from the magazines and turns them into *pinnspetsknytning* (sprang work). When she saw a cross-stitch pattern in a magazine depicting an angel, she enlarged it and now has a whole collection of sprang angels.

"That's the sort of thing people want to buy, but I won't sell my angels! I used to paint and weave for almost every farm around here, but now I do all the sprang I can find time for. Sprang has been used for a lot of things—cushions and pillows, window ledges, lampshades, shawls, and bags. I don't do anything at all with mine—except put them in the windows, of course. They're just the thing for the older houses here."

"Sprang" is sewn on a network of woven threads. The meshes are lozenge-shaped. If they are straight, the technique is called Gepür. The basic work is done with needles and a measuring stick (to gauge the size of the holes), and is then rigged up on a wooden frame or pinned to a board. 1985.

Elin Vinge.

The pattern is sewn with loosely twisted linen yarn, using a "darning stitch" which is sewn in both directions, just like darning socks. When the work is finished it is removed from the frame, sprayed with starch and pressed.

A sprang-worked star resplendent in the front-door window of Elin Vinge's house.

AGNETA SPÅNGBERG

POTTER

A trade journal referred to a Functionalist service from Uppsala-Ekeby by saying that it had "a slight touch of madness." This seems a very apt comment on Agneta Spångberg's tea-service as well, with its extraordinary shapes and colors. The serious-minded feel immediately compeled to ask whether she is joking. Can you make jokes with utility objects? And if you do, is the result a useful item or a work of art? The answers lie in the eye of the beholder. The potter, through her work, asks the question.

In America, Agneta Spångberg's ceramic ware has been dubbed "New Wave" in its color and design, while in Sweden she has been told that she makes "Pippi Longstocking pottery," "Alice in Wonderland pottery," and that she represents a style "far removed from classical good taste." Agneta, who trained at Capellagården in Sweden and the Sun Valley Center for the Arts in America, says that her classical training in pottery and more flexible training in expressive ceramic design have been useful to her. In Sweden the artists are confined by a straitjacket of "good taste," while in the States no holds are barred!

"Today I couldn't imagine living without the tension, the excitement that these two traditions have given me. A mug has to be practical, but it must also express something. I like it when the décor is electrically charged, while the form remains simple. I'm looking for a combination of sophistication and play, and I'm not afraid to say that I don't want the function to impair the appearance."

Agneta, who has spent several seasons working in America, uses both earthenware and stoneware firing in an electric kiln, and sometimes she also uses raku-firing. She spent three summers working with archaeologists at the Eketorp Prehistoric Fort on the island of Öland. By studying potsherds from the Iron Age, digging clay near the fort, and working with a reconstructed kiln built from turves and fired with twigs and cow dung, she eventually came up with a kind of pottery which, according to art historians, very closely resembles the original. Talk about getting back to basics!

Agneta is also inspired by fabrics, flowers, and movies. "My quintessentially Swedish ego benefits enormously from exploring in America. I enjoy looking at shocking-pink antacid medicine, tinted popcorn, electric knives, winking holiday lights in caramel colors, layer cakes with whole tiers of plastic and cake mixture, and plastic-wrapped pastries in pastel colors guaranteed to stay fresh for twelve years . . ."

At one time Agneta produced pottery in delicate pastel shades, at another she experimented a great deal with checked patterns for everyday objects. Today her glazes are very colorful and she has added "purely decorative" dishes and trays to her everyday pottery.

"Unconventional clashes of color fascinate me, the sort of thing you can see in a Mexican market or an American supermarket. But the craftsmanship, the solidity, is Swedish."

Two raku-fired mugs, black and white with orange-striped handles. The cups, of porcelain clay, are thrown on the wheel and fired at a low 950°. The cracking from the raku firing makes every mug unique. 1984.

Agneta Spångberg.

The Razzia *tea service, earthenware thrown on the wheel and fired at 1,050°. This service consists of a teapot, sugar bowl, jug, tray, and cups and saucers. The dry clay has been cast, fired to biscuit temperature, and then glazed with a transparent glaze and red glaze for the handles. The matte, bluish-gray effect was achieved with a mixture of slip and sand. 1986.*

LENA EKLUND

PAINTER

Lena Eklund has worked with design for 25 years. Together with her husband Al she has worked for both Swedish and Danish companies, designing children's clothing (Lollipop), stockings, household articles, notepaper, and so forth. For 20 years she has been living at "Skånegården" near Förslöv in Skåne, with five cats to keep her company. She has given up design and is now painting because the two have gone their separate ways.

"I got fed up with products having to be changed all the time, even when they were good. The commercial world wants new things all the time, and I think good things should be allowed to go on and on."

Good things for Lena include her home at "Skånegården," where she can walk barefoot outdoors in the morning, close to the sea and to her cats.

"I sometimes think that the cats really own this house, and I'm just the lodger. Melissa has lived here for 17 years and exploits me in an affectionate sort of way for food, warmth, and occasionally something soft to sit on. I try to live more simply, more distinctly and independently, the way my cats do, but with a very clear feeling of being at home. I paint cats and other things I like as distinctly as I can. I'm not an intellectual painter; somebody once said that I was a purist painter, but definitely I am not a puritan."

Lena Eklund sells her work through exhibitions and to private customers. Otherwise she makes a living helping local people with such practical tasks as painting walls, reupholstering furniture, clearing weeds, and all the other jobs that have to be done in a home and garden. She alternates between practical work and painting, out of an increasingly apparent need to stay close to her farm and her cats.

"Sometimes I can sit and paint all day—it's pure meditation. I aim at purity of feeling. Not the ascetically strict and denuded kind, but what is pure, abundant, sensual, and good. There is happiness painting a bright red coffee pot or a black cat with a fish between its paws. That's real love."

In *Cats*, Doris Lessing says that a cat needs a home of its own just as much as it needs a person it can call its own. In addition to a home, some people need a cat (or several) that they can call their own.

Lena Eklund, with two models.

Lena Eklund and her cats live in a late-18th-century farmhouse.

White cat, 1983.

Black-and-white cat, 1983.

Moo-cow, 1982.

Lena lives in the heart of the countryside, surrounded by a variety of models.

MARGARETA NORENIUS-BERGLUND

WEAVER

Is weaving rag rugs "art"? And is there any art to it? The answer, of course, is yes. It is time that the tradition of women re-using textiles to make new mats was given the appreciation it deserves, and was considered to be art.

"This rug is my life," says Margareta Norenius-Berglund. "It has textiles in it all the way from my childhood. Dad's striped pajamas, Mum's flower-patterned housecoat, my best friend's party dress, and my daughters' baby clothes. I'm like a squirrel: the attic's full of bags with things I can't bring myself to throw away. Sometimes I get still more bags of old clothes from friends who know that I tear them up for rag rugs."

Margareta weaves for the crafts center in Leksand, producing both the traditional patterns and the most beautiful "ordinary" rag rugs. She tears or cuts strips, often 1 to 2 centimetres wide, depending on the thickness of the cloth. Before she can start weaving there's the business of warping and setting up the weave. "You can't make a living out of weaving; you may get 10 or so kronor an hour for it, which is why handwoven mats are harder and harder to come by." Art fabrics command completely different prices, but traditional weaving is not yet as valuable.

"So you weave just for the pleasure and to see that this primeval woman's chore doesn't just disappear. I actually only learned it six years ago, and I'm sort of in a hurry to make up for all the years when I didn't weave. It feels as if I have at last found a use for my hands and feelings in one single context. I think of nothing but weaving—it's so exciting my hands can hardly keep up."

If you want to care for your rag rugs so that they will improve with age, just follow this old Finnish recipe. Rag rugs should be scrubbed by hand, down by the lakeside, one day when the weather is fine. You take a bucket, brush, soft soap, dirty rugs, and a picnic basket with you, as well as the neighbor's wife, a few grown men to carry the wet rugs, and of course the kids. Then you scrub and chat and drink coffee all day on the jetty. When you put the rugs out to dry, you have to hang them up lengthwise on the line, so that the water from the more colorful stripes won't stain the pale ones.

Rosepath weave, a traditional pattern, woven by Margareta Norenius-Berglund.

Page 179: Detail of rag rug. Margareta Norenius-Berglund has turned "family rags" into genuine rag rugs. This one contains "strips of Dad's pajamas, my best friend's old party dress, and my daughters' baby clothes."

Margareta Norenius-Berglund.

Margareta lives in Leksand, Dalarna, as you may guess from the colors of this rag rug.

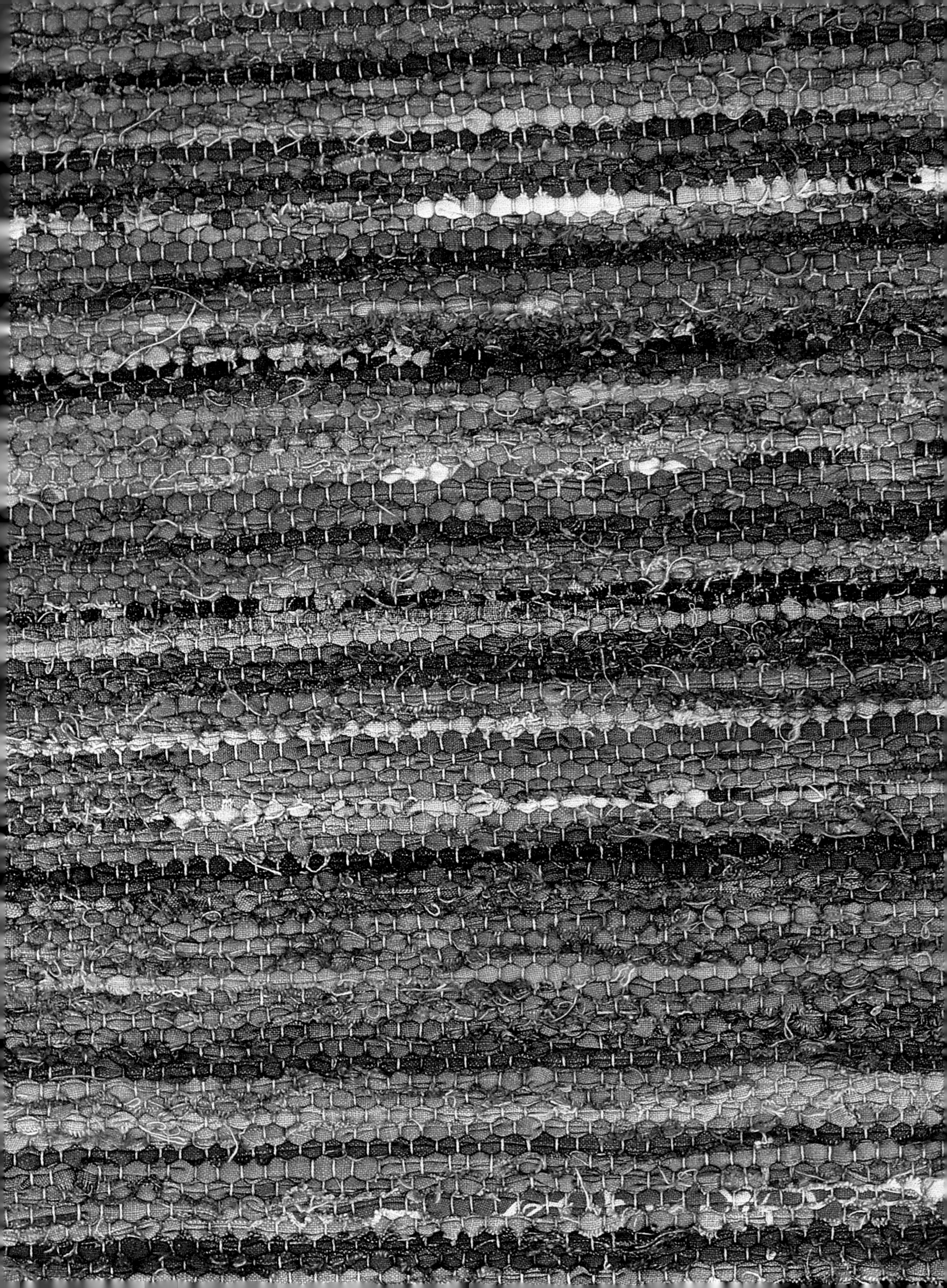

ULRICA HYDMAN-VALLIEN

GLASS DESIGNER

"'Do something *properly*, Ulrica, something that won't annoy people,' they say to me. But I have to do things with a flourish—it's good for me," says Ulrica cheerfully. "I have to make unusual decorations, gorging myself on the world I enjoy. It's like when I was small, really. I used to draw fantasy figures and animals with faces—like the serpents I do today. Of course my conceptual world has changed, and my animals today are more bizarre, and my pictures of women perhaps ironic."

Ulrica divides her activities into utility ware and studio pieces, with a décor that sometimes provides information, sometimes a message, but is often purely decorative. She worked as a potter after her studies at the National College of Art and Design, and not until she was approached by the Orrefors Glassworks did she begin to design glass. Previously she felt the material to be less important than her need to express herself, but after 14 years of working with glass she is beginning to be fascinated by the molten glass itself.

"Glass invites you to express yourself rather grandly, elegantly, and strictly, and I've felt the need to be a bit provocative. I was once commissioned to make a really traditional Swedish fiftieth-birthday present, a bowl. So I made this dreadful great bowl with pink-tongued rats climbing all over it. Nobody liked it or bought it. Except me. I'm terribly fond of things that I've made myself—once I've done a thing, I can never change it. I think I'm lazy, even if I am always working. Over the years I've come to accept that I have an immensely direct way of working, instinctively, head-on."

Some people find Ulrica's glass provocative, and a sufficient number love it. Ulrica has been awarded fellowships and design prizes in Sweden, Germany, and the United States. She has exhibited in Brazil, the United States, France, Germany and, of course, Sweden; and she is represented in museums as far away as Japan.

"Just now I'm doing paintings in glass sculptures. First I decorate a glass egg which is heated up and fastened to the blow-pipe, and then you blow air into the egg, which enlarges it so that the decorations grow into new shapes. Then you dip the new shape several times into clear crystal. As long as the ball is kept moving the décor changes, and it doesn't settle until the glass solidifies. It's absolutely wonderful then, and it turns out a bit mysterious almost, just the way I want it."

Ulrica Hydman-Vallien behind her glass painting of fantasy figures.

180

Serpent Goblets, *part of a series for Kosta Boda, 1978.*

Blue vase in jewel technique, inner layer of blue, outer layer of green, sand-blasted and enameled. Kosta Boda, 1985.

Bluish-gray frosted bowl, enameled bottle glass. Kosta Boda, 1985.

PERSONAL INDEX

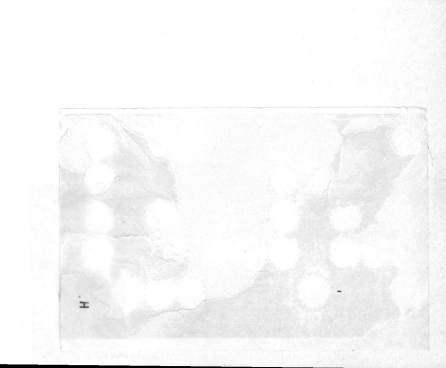